# ANGELA'S ASHES

Frank McCourt

LEVEL 3

SCHOLASTIC

**'Angela's Ashes' adapted by:** Jane Rollason

**Fact Files written by:** Jacquie Bloese

**Commissioning Editor:** Jacquie Bloese

**Editor:** Matthew Hancock

**Cover design:** Dawn Wilson

**Designer:** Dawn Wilson

**Picture research:** Emma Bree and Osha Mason

**Photo credits:**
**Cover:** Culver Pictures. **Page 4:** Culver Pictures; Limerick City Museum; Hulton Duetsch/Corbis.
**Page 5:** I. Underhill, J. & L. Merill, E. O Hoppé/Corbis.
**Page 6:** Bettmann/Corbis. **Page 14:** Digital Vision.
**Page 15:** Limerick City Museum. **Page 22:** Limerick City Museum. **Page 25:** Limerick City Museum.
**Page 35:** Bettmann/Corbis. **Page 44:** A. Holt/Alamy.
**Page 46:** Limerick City Museum. **Page 59:** Limerick City Museum. **Page 71:** Limerick City Museum.
**Page 77:** Limerick City Museum. **Page 79:** W. Little/Getty Images. **Page 80:** E. Feferberg; AFP/Getty Images; Sygma/Corbis. **Page 81:** Sygma/Corbis.
**Page 82:** Sygma/Corbis. **Page 83:** Sygma/Corbis.
**Pages 84 & 85:** Chromepix.com/Alamy; PA/Empics; R. Wallis/Corbis.

Published by arrangement with HarperCollins Publishers Ltd.

Mary Glasgow Magazines (Scholastic Ltd.)
Euston House
24 Eversholt Street
London NW1 IDB

Printed in Singapore. Reprinted in 2009.
This edition printed in 2010.

# CONTENTS

## FRANK McCOURT

Frank McCourt was born in New York, USA in 1930, but his parents were from Ireland. Frank is short for Francis. People also call him Frankie.

## ANGELA (SHEEHAN) McCOURT

Frank's mother was born in a poor lane in Limerick in the south of Ireland. She never saw her father, who ran off to Australia before she was born. She went to school until she was nine. Then she tried working for a rich family, but she wasn't very good at it. Her mother told her she was useless and sent her to America for work and a better life.

## MALACHY McCOURT

Frank's father, Malachy, was born on a farm in the North of Ireland. When he was young, he was wild and he fought for the IRA against the English (see pages 84–85). He got into trouble and had to escape from Ireland; he went to America.

The Irish Republican Army, 1920

## This is part of Frank's family tree:

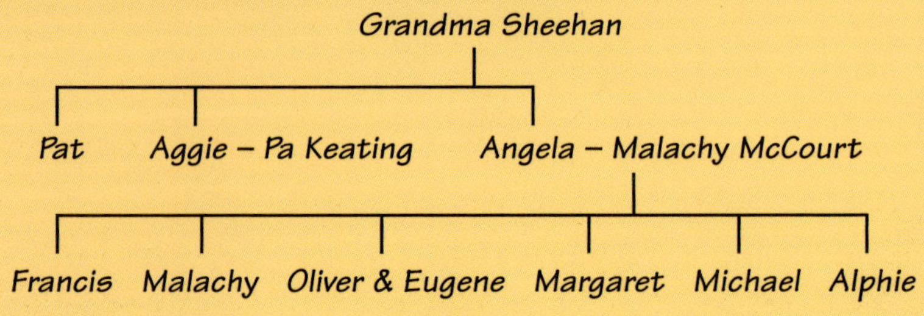

## New York

The McCourts lived in Brooklyn, New York in the 1930s, when it was very hard to get a job and people were very poor. It was against the law to buy, sell or drink alcohol, but there were secret bars and clubs where you could get alcohol. Malachy often visited these.

## Limerick

The family moved to Limerick in the South of Ireland because there was no work in America. But they found there was no work in Limerick either.

Limerick is a very wet place next to the Atlantic Ocean. Great rain clouds come up the River Shannon and empty over the city. The poor people in Frank's time lived in cold, wet houses and many became very ill. The only warm, dry place was inside the church. Limerick was the most religious place in Ireland!

## The Catholic Church

When Frank McCourt was growing up, the Catholic Church was very powerful in Ireland. People were more afraid of the priests than of the police.

Frank is eight when he prepares for First Communion. He has to learn questions and answers about the Catholic religion, he has to practise taking the wafer and wine (the body and blood of Jesus) and he has to tell the priest his sins (the things he has done wrong). If he doesn't tell the priest his sins, he believes he will go to hell.

Frank is ten when he has to learn more questions and answers for confirmation. When he is confirmed, he can become a full member of the Church.

# Angela's Ashes

## PROLOGUE

New York, 1930

An unhappy childhood is bad enough. An unhappy Irish childhood is worse. But an unhappy Irish Catholic childhood is the worst of all.

My unhappy Irish Catholic childhood started in New York, on Thanksgiving Day during the Great Depression*. My mother, Angela Sheehan, had just arrived from Ireland. She met Malachy McCourt at a Thanksgiving party. Malachy liked Angela, and she liked him. She thought he looked sad. He did, because he'd just spent three months in prison. He and his friend John had stolen a lorry. They thought it was full of boxes of tinned meat. Neither of them could drive and the lorry was going from

* In the early 1930s, many people in the US and Europe couldn't find a job and were very poor.

side to side on the road. So the police stopped them and searched the lorry. There was no tinned meat.

'Why have you stolen a lorry that's full of empty boxes?' the police asked them.

Angela felt sorry for Malachy and Malachy was feeling lonely after his time in prison … Well, my life started at that Thanksgiving party.

Angela had cousins in New York. Their names were Delia and Philomena. They were good Irish Catholics from Limerick and they knew what was right and what was wrong. And it was wrong to be expecting a child when you weren't married.

With their husbands behind them, they went to a drinking club on Atlantic Avenue. The man in the club didn't want to let them in.

'Do you want to keep the nose on your face?' asked Philomena.

'We're here on God's business,' said Delia.

'All right, all right,' he said. 'You Irish are trouble.'

Malachy was sitting at the bar. When he saw them, he went white. He gave them a weak smile and offered them a drink.

'You people from the North of Ireland are different from us in the South,' Delia said. 'You have a strange look. And you are a disgrace to the Irish people for what you did to our cousin.'

'Oh, I am,' said Malachy, 'I am.'

'Nobody asked your opinion,' said Philomena.

'You're going to marry that girl,' said Delia.

'I wasn't planning to get married, you know. There's no work and how could I …?'

He saw the look on their faces. They were ready to eat him alive.

Angela Sheehan and Malachy McCourt married on a very cold day in March. I was born in August. They took me to church to name me Francis after my father's father and the lovely saint of Assisi. Malachy had a drink before he came to the church. The priest said something about the whisky and Malachy got angry and wanted to fight him.

'Quiet, man,' said the priest, 'you're in God's house.' And when Malachy said, 'God's house, my arse*,' the priest threw him out of the church. You can't say 'arse' in God's house.

Philomena gave a party after church with tea, sandwiches and cakes.

'Tea?' said Malachy.

'Yes, tea. You won't find whisky in this house.'

'Tea is fine,' said Malachy, 'I just need to go out for a minute.' They knew what he meant.

'Your son's special day and you have to go drinking!' cried Philomena and Delia.' You're a disgrace to your family!'

At Philomena's house, Angela sat in the corner with the baby, crying. Philomena piled her plate with cakes.

'Why did you do it, Angela? You're just off the boat from Ireland and you marry that madman.'

Angela cried harder.

'It's your own fault. He's a drunk from the North. He doesn't even look like a Catholic,' said Delia.

'Make sure there are no more children, Angela. He doesn't have a job. He never will have a job because he drinks too much. Are you listening, Angela?'

'I am, Philomena.'

A year later, my brother Malachy was born.

'We'll never speak to her again,' said the cousins.

* A rude word for *bottom*.

# CHAPTER 1
## New York

One day, Malachy and I are playing in the park – jumping on some bits of wood. I jump too hard and Malachy screams. There's blood everywhere. We run back to the flat. Dad's out looking for a job but Mam's there. She takes one look at Malachy and the blood pouring out of his mouth.

'Jesus, Mary and Joseph,' she cries, and she runs to the hospital with him.

Now I'm on my own at home. I walk between the two rooms – the bedroom and the kitchen. There's nothing to eat in the ice box. I fall asleep on my parents' bed. When my mother wakes me up, it's nearly dark.

'Your little brother needs to sleep,' she says. 'He nearly bit his tongue off. Go into the other room.'

My father is in the kitchen, drinking black tea from his big white cup. 'Come and sit here,' he says. He tells me a good Northern Irish story. He gives me some of his black tea. It tastes horrible, but I'm happy sitting there.

For days Malachy can't talk because of his tongue. But no one notices him anyway because we have two new babies.

Malachy and I play in the park because of the babies. Malachy laughs all the time and his tongue gets better. When he laughs you can see his pretty white teeth. He has blue eyes like Mam, and golden hair and pink skin. I have brown eyes, black hair and white skin like Dad. My mother tells our neighbour Mrs Liebowitz that Malachy is the happiest child in the world. She says Frankie has the strange look like his father. I want to know what the strange look is. I can't ask because I shouldn't be listening.

***

I wish I could fly up into the clouds. Then I wouldn't hear my two brothers, Eugene and Oliver, crying in the night. My mother says they're always hungry. She cries in the night, too. She says four boys is too much for her and she'd like one little girl all for herself.

Dad is out looking for a job again. Sometimes when he comes home, he smells of whisky. He sings songs about poor old Ireland. Mam gets angry and says Ireland can kiss her arse. He says that's nice language to use in front of the children. She says she doesn't care about the language, she wants food on the table and not poor old Ireland.

Prohibition* has ended now. Dad gets jobs in bars. He washes the floor and gets a whisky or a beer. Sometimes he brings bits of food from the bars. He puts the food on the table but drinks tea himself. He never eats. He says food upsets his stomach.

When Dad gets a good job, Mam smiles and sings. When he brings home a week's money on the first Friday of the new job, she can pay the lovely Italian man in the shop on the corner. She cleans the kitchen. She heats water and washes us and Dad dries us. We have tea and bread and potatoes with butter and salt. Dad tells us stories and shows us letters and words in the *Daily News,* or he smokes a cigarette and looks out of the window.

But if Dad's job lasts into the third week, he doesn't bring home the money. We wait for him on Friday night. The darkness comes and the lights go on along Classon Avenue. Other men with jobs are home already and having dinner. You can hear the families talking, you can

*During Prohibition (1920-33), people were not allowed to buy, sell or drink whisky or beer.

smell the eggs frying, you can hear the music on the radios.

Malachy and I play with Eugene and Oliver. Mam doesn't sing. She sits at the kitchen table, smoking a cigarette, drinking tea and crying. I want to tell her I'll be a man soon and get a job and I'll come home every Friday night with the money. Much later, Dad comes up the stairs singing Irish songs.

'Where are my four Irishmen?' he shouts. 'Get up, boys. Stand up and promise to die for Ireland.'

'Leave those boys alone,' says Mam. Her face is wet. 'Jesus, Mary and Joseph, it's bad enough to come home without any money in your pocket and with whisky in your stomach,' she says to him. 'Go back to bed,' she says to us.

'I want them up,' he shouts. 'They must be ready for the day Ireland is free from Dublin to the sea.' The next week he loses his job.

And then there's a new baby, a little girl, and they call her Margaret. We all love Margaret. She has soft black hair and blue eyes like Mam. Mrs Liebowitz says the world never saw such eyes or such a smile.

Dad walks round the kitchen with her and talks to her. He tells her how lovely she is.

'I'll take you to Ireland and show you the beautiful countryside. I'll get a job soon, I will, and you'll have pretty dresses and shoes.' The more Dad sings to Margaret, the less she cries. Mam says, 'Look at him dancing with that child, him with his two left feet.'

'He's in heaven over that child,' Mam tells Mrs Liebowitz. 'He hasn't had a drink since she was born. I wish I'd had a girl a long time ago.'

***

It's early in the morning. My mother's whispering.

'What's up with the child?' she says. Dad's by the window with Margaret in his arms. 'Is she sick?' Mam says.

'She's very quiet and a bit cold,' says Dad

'Go for the doctor, for God's sake,' says Mam.

When Dad comes back with the doctor, he smells of whisky. The doctor looks at the baby. He feels her neck, arms, legs. He shakes his head. 'She's gone,' he says. Mam holds the baby close, turns to the wall.

The doctor says he'll have to take the baby's body to the hospital and Dad signs a paper. Mam has a wild look, her hair is wet, her face is shiny with tears. 'Jesus, Mary and Joseph,' she cries, 'help me!'

Eugene and Oliver are awake. They're crying with hunger. Mam doesn't move or make a sound. Dad's face is white. He hits his legs with his hands. Then he puts his hand on my head. 'Francis,' he says to me, 'I'm going out for cigarettes.'

Malachy and I give our brothers water and sugar. I find some old bread and mix it with milk and we eat it.

Mrs Liebowitz comes to see us. 'Oh, Mrs McCourt, what's the matter? Look at the little ones. No clothes on and dirty bottoms. Is the baby sick?' My mother doesn't answer.

She helps my mother to sit up. She goes to get some soup. Mam holds my hand tight. I'm frightened. I've never seen her like this.

'Your lovely little sister is dead, Frankie. And where is your father? Drinking. He can't get a job but he finds money for the drink.' She screams, 'Where is she? Where is she? Oh, Jesus, Mary and Joseph, I'll go mad.'

Mrs Liebowitz runs back in with the soup. 'What is it? Where's the little girl?'

My mother screams again, 'Dead. Seven weeks in this world, Mrs Liebowitz.'

Mrs Liebowitz holds my mother in her arms. 'It happens, my love. God takes them.'

'What is God going to do with little babies?'

'I don't know, my love. Have some soup. It's good soup. It'll make you strong. Boys, have some soup.'

The soup is lovely and hot. I wonder if Mrs Liebowitz could be my mother. I wish little Margaret could be here for the soup.

I hear Mrs Liebowitz talking to another neighbour. 'Where are Mrs McCourt's cousins?' she asks her. 'The big women with the quiet husbands? I'll find them. I'll tell them the children are wild, with sore arses.'

Two days later, Dad's back from his cigarette search. It's the middle of the night. He smells of whisky and he gets me and Malachy out of bed.

'You'll die for Ireland, won't you, boys?'

'We will, Dad.'

'And we'll meet your little sister in heaven, won't we, boys?'

'We will, Dad.'

***

Two big women are at the door. They say their names are Philomena and Delia.

'Who are you?' they ask me.

'I'm Frank.'

'Frank! How old are you?'

'Four.'

'You're not very big for your age, are you?'

They walk past me into the room. 'Jesus, Mary and Joseph, this place smells awful. And who are these children?'

Malachy runs up with a big smile. The big women smile back. I wonder why they didn't smile at me.

Mrs Liebowitz comes in and the three women sit at the table. 'These children are a disgrace,' they say. 'We'll write a letter.'

Ellis Island

They wrote to Grandma Sheehan, Angela's mother in Limerick. When she got the letter, she sent money to Philomena and Delia. They bought the tickets for Ireland and put us on the ship in Manhattan. They said, 'Goodbye and don't come back.'

The ship set out to sea. Mam said, 'That's the Statue of Liberty and that's Ellis Island,' as we went by. Then she put her head over the side and was sick. The wind blew the sick all over us. 'Jesus, Mary and Joseph,' said the people standing behind us, and they went inside.

# CHAPTER 2
## Limerick

A week later we arrived in Limerick. Grandma Sheehan met us on the station platform. She had white hair, mean eyes and black clothes. She didn't smile at any of us. Mam introduced Dad.

Limerick Station

'This is Malachy McCourt,' she said. Grandma looked at him and looked away. She called two boys over. They had shaved heads, dirty noses and no shoes. She paid them to carry our suitcase. Dad carried Eugene and Oliver. Mam carried a bag in one hand and held little Malachy's hand in the other. She stopped every few minutes for a rest, and Grandma said, 'Are you still smoking those cigarettes? Those cigarettes will kill you. There's enough consumption in Limerick already without people smoking as well.'

***

Grandma's house is in a narrow lane. On her kitchen wall there is a picture of a man with long brown hair and sad eyes. His heart is burning.

'That's the Sacred Heart of Jesus*,' says Mam.

'Why is the man's heart on fire?' I ask. 'And why doesn't he throw water on it?'

'Don't these children know anything about their religion?' asks Grandma.

'It's different in America,' says Mam.

And Grandma says that the Sacred Heart is everywhere and that's no excuse.

Grandma makes tea and tells Mam to cut the bread but not too thick. There aren't enough chairs for everyone, so I sit on the stairs with my brothers.

'I don't know what I'm going to do with ye*,' Grandma says. 'There's no room for ye in this house. There's me and your brother Pat already.'

Malachy says, 'Ye, ye,' and starts laughing. I say 'Ye, ye,' and Eugene and Oliver say 'Ye, ye.' We're laughing so much that we can't eat our bread. Grandma looks hard at us. 'What are ye laughing at? There's nothing to laugh at in this house.'

***

That day Grandma and Mam found a room for us on Windmill Street. Mam's sister Aunt Aggie had a flat there with her husband Uncle Pa Keating. Aunt Aggie is big like Delia and Philomena, and she has red hair. She doesn't smile either.

Grandma paid for the room for the first two weeks. She gave Mam money for food, cooking pots, knives, spoons and cups. 'That's all I can give you,' she said. 'He'll have to get off his arse and get a job,' she said, looking at Dad. 'Or you can go to the St Vincent de Paul Society*.'

*Grandma's picture shows Jesus with his heart burning. When she looks at it, she thinks of Jesus's love for her and all people.
*A Limerick word for 'you'.
*A Catholic charity that gave food and clothes to the poor.

The room had a fireplace. We could heat water for our tea or an egg if we ever became rich. We had a table, three chairs and the biggest bed Mam had ever seen. All six of us slept on that bed. It was lovely after three nights on Grandma's floor. And we could laugh and say 'ye' as much as we liked.

In the night, Eugene screamed. He sat up and tore at his skin. We all started screaming. Dad turned on the gaslight and we saw the fleas. They were biting us all, jumping from body to body. We jumped out of bed. 'Oh Jesus, will we have no rest?' said Mam.

They say that the English brought the fleas to Ireland to drive the Irish mad. Before that, it was a lovely place. We slept on the floor by the fire for the rest of the night.

***

A few days later Dad wakes me. 'Run over to your Aunt Aggie,' he says. 'Your mother needs her. Hurry!'

I run across the street and knock on her door. Uncle Pa Keating comes out coughing. 'What's up?'

'I think my mother's sick.'

'Ye are nothing but trouble since ye came from America,' says Aunt Aggie.

'Leave him alone,' says Uncle Pa, 'he's only a child.'

Everyone whispers when we get back. I can just hear Aunt Aggie tell Uncle Pa the child is lost. I wonder what child is lost because we're all here: one, two, three, four of us. A man comes and takes Mam to hospital. There's blood on the floor. I want to ask Dad if Mam is going forever, like my sister Margaret. But Dad goes with Mam, and you can't ask Aunt Aggie anything. She just gets cross.

Mam is soon home, though, and Dad goes for the dole*.

*Money paid by the government every week to families with no jobs.

He can't get a job because he's from the North of Ireland. All the jobs go to the Limerick men. He comes home and says we're getting nineteen shillings* a week.

'Nineteen shillings for six of us?' says Mam. 'The room costs five shillings. That leaves fourteen shillings for food and clothes and coal to heat the water for tea.'

Dad doesn't answer. Instead he sings an Irish song and Eugene and Oliver dance. Mam looks into the ashes in the fireplace, and you can see the worry in her face.

The next day, Mam takes Malachy and me to the St Vincent de Paul Society. We wait in a line with women wearing black. They smile when we talk.

'God above, listen to the little Yankees*,' they say. 'There isn't enough for the poor people of Limerick without Yanks coming over and taking the bread out of our mouths.'

Mam tells them our story and cries when she talks about Margaret. The women cry too, then. They know that there's nothing worse in the world than losing a child.

When it's our turn, they call us in. Mam, Malachy and I stand in front of a table with three men. She tells them her story and starts crying again about Margaret. The man in the middle gives her a ticket for tea, sugar, milk and butter from Mrs McGrath's shop. There's another ticket for coal from Dock Road.

'You won't be getting this every week,' says the man on the right. 'We'll be visiting your house to see if there's a real need.'

'God will thank you for your kindness,' she says. The men look at the table, the ceiling and the walls, and tell her to send in the next woman.

*Irish money at this time was pounds, shillings and pence.
*Colloquial for an American; not very polite.

# CHAPTER 3
# Oliver and Eugene

We get home and Oliver is sitting on Dad's knee. His face is bright red and he's looking at the ashes of the dead fire. Dad's telling him a story but he's not listening.

'He's not well,' says Mam. 'He's hot.' She gives Dad the ticket from the St Vincent de Paul for the coal. 'We need a fire,' she says. 'To heat some milk for Oliver.'

Dad and I go down to Dock Road. But it's dark and closed. Women and small children are picking up coal that's dropped from lorries onto the road.

'There, Dad. There's coal.' I point.

'Oh, no, son. We won't pick coal off the road. We're not beggars.'

He tells Mam everything is closed. When I tell her about the coal on the road, she gets up.

'If you're too proud to pick up coal, I'm not.' She gets a bag and takes me and Malachy with her. The other women have gone. We fill our bag with bits of coal. We pick up anything that burns – coal, wood, paper.

Dad is walking up and down with Oliver when we get back. We show him the coal.

'Oh, I knew you'd get the coal,' he says. 'I said a prayer to St Jude. He's the saint for people with nothing.'

'I got the coal,' says Mam, 'with no help from St Jude.'

'You shouldn't pick up coal from Dock Road like a beggar. It isn't right. It's a bad example for the boys,' he replies.

'Then you should have sent St Jude down to Dock Road.'

Malachy says he's hungry and I'm hungry too. But we have to wait while Mam heats milk for Oliver. She tries to feed him but he turns away and looks at the fire. She puts him to bed.

She fries some bread. We sit round the fire and eat it and drink hot sweet tea. The fire makes the room warm. We turn off the light to save the gas. The fire makes shapes all round the room and we watch them dance.

Soon we're all in bed. The room goes red and black till the fire dies. Then all you can hear is a little cry from Oliver in Mam's arms.

The next morning Mam and Dad put a coat round Oliver and take him to the hospital. When they're gone, Eugene sits on the bed and looks out of the window.

'Ollie, Ollie,' he says. 'I want Ollie.'

Malachy and I make tea and bread with sugar, but Eugene won't eat it.

Grandma is at the door. I tell her about Oliver and Eugene.

'That child looks hungry,' she says. 'Have ye any porridge here?'

'What's porridge?' says Malachy.

'Jesus, Mary and Joseph! What's porridge! Ye are the stupidest Yanks I've ever seen. Come on. We'll go across the street to your Aunt Aggie. She'll give ye porridge.'

'Do ye have any porridge?' Grandma says to Aunt Aggie.

'Porridge? Do I have to give porridge to a crowd of Yanks now?'

'It won't kill ye to give them a bit of porridge,' says Grandma.

'They'll be wanting sugar and milk on top of their porridge, will they?'

'It's a good thing you didn't own the stable in Bethlehem*,' says Grandma.

*The innkeeper in Bethlehem let Mary and Joseph stay in the stable with the cows when the inn was full. Jesus was born in the stable.

Uncle Pa comes in. He has black hair and his skin is black. I like his eyes because they're very blue and ready to smile.

'Why are you all black?' asks Malachy.

Uncle Pa laughs and says, 'I'm black because I work at the Limerick Gas Works. I was gassed in France in the war* and now I'm gassed every day in Limerick.' Uncle Pa puts Eugene on his knee. 'You've got a sad little face,' he says, and makes funny faces and sounds. Eugene laughs.

'I think he likes me,' says Uncle Pa.

Aunt Aggie suddenly puts down her teacup and cries loudly.

'Aw, Jesus, Aggie,' says Grandma. 'What's the matter with ye this time?'

'Pa there with a child,' she cries, 'when I can't have a child of my own. There's Angela with five born and one dead. And she can't even keep a room clean. And I can clean and cook as well as anyone.'

'Don't talk like that in front of the children,' says Grandma. 'When God's ready He'll send ye a family.'

Uncle Pa laughs at Eugene. 'I think I'll keep this one.'

Malachy and I run to him. 'No, no, you can't,' we say, 'That's our brother.'

'I don't want anything of Angela's,' says Aggie. 'I don't want something that's half North of Ireland and half Limerick. I'll have my own one day.'

Later we go home and fall asleep. When I wake up, Mam is making small crying sounds like a bird. Dad is hitting his legs with his hands.

'Oh, Francis, your little brother Oliver is dead. Your little sister is dead.' He laughs like a mad man. Then he picks me up and holds me so tight I cry out.

*World War I (1914-18).

'Come on, Francis. We'll find food for a wonderful meal,' he says.

He carries me through the streets of Limerick. We go from shop to shop and ask for food for a family that's lost two children in a year. Most shopkeepers say sorry, but no, and tell us to go to the St Vincent de Paul.

'It's good to see that Christ is alive in Limerick today,' says Dad.

'We don't need people from the North to tell us about Christ,' they say.

A few shopkeepers give us bread, potatoes, tins of beans. On the way home we meet Pa Keating. Uncle Pa buys Dad a pint in South's pub for his troubles. Other men in the pub buy Dad pints. Soon he's singing Irish songs.

South's pub

'I think you've had enough now, mister,' says the man behind the bar. 'We're sorry for your troubles, but you must take that boy home to his mother.'

Dad wants just one more pint and starts to fight when he doesn't get it. Uncle Pa takes us home.

The next day they put Oliver in a white box. They put

the box in the ground and cover it with earth. The day after that, Dad drinks the dole money again and we don't have anything to eat.

***

The next week Malachy and I start at Leamy's National School.

On the first day there's a fight because the boys call us cowboys and gangsters*. One of the teachers, Mr Benson, pulls me out of the fight.

'Is that what you do in America? Hold out your hand,' he says, and hits it hard with a stick. 'Say after me, "I'm a bad Yank".'

'I'm a bad Yank.'

'He's not a bad Yank,' says Malachy. 'It's that big boy. He said we were cowboys and gangsters.'

'Is that what you did, Heffernan?'

'I was only joking, sir.'

'No more joking, Heffernan. It's not their fault that they're Yanks.'

'It isn't, sir.'

'If you were a Yank, Heffernan, you'd be worse than Al Capone. If you call these two names again, I'll hang your skin on the wall.'

There are seven teachers at Leamy's. They all have leather belts and sticks. They hit you on the shoulders, the back, the legs and the hands. They hit you if you're late, if you talk, if you laugh. They hit you if you don't know the saint of Limerick, if you can't find Bulgaria on the map, if you can't add nineteen to forty-seven.

The older boys tell us about the teachers, what they like and what they hate. Mr Benson hates America and you

*Jesse James was a famous cowboy and Al Capone was a famous gangster.

have to remember to hate America or he'll hit you. Mr O'Dea hates England and you have to remember to hate England or he'll hit you.

Even if they hit you six times on each hand with their longest stick, you must not cry. There are boys who might laugh if you cry. But they have to be careful, too. One day it will be their turn and they must not cry or the other boys will laugh at them even more. And it's no use telling your mother or father. They always say, 'Don't be a baby.'

***

Every morning when Eugene wakes up, he looks for Ollie under the bed or behind the chair. He points at children in the street with fair hair like Ollie and calls him, 'Ollie, Ollie!' He doesn't understand that Ollie is in heaven with Margaret. He's only two.

Malachy and I play with him. We try to make him laugh.

'He'll forget Ollie soon, with God's help,' says Dad.

Six months later, Eugene died anyway.

Dr Troy came. 'This child was very sick,' he said. 'Why wasn't he in the hospital long ago?'

'We didn't know,' said Mam and Dad.

'If the other boys have even a little cough, you must bring them to me, day or night,' he says. 'Keep them dry at all times. I'm very sorry for your troubles, Mrs McCourt. Here's something to help the pain of the days to come,' he said. He shook his head. 'God is asking too much, too much.'

# CHAPTER 4
## Upstairs in Italy

Mam says that she can't spend another minute in that room on Windmill Street. She sees Eugene morning and night. She sees him on the bed looking out of the window for Oliver.

Roden Lane

We move to a house in Roden Lane. The houses are called 'two up, two down' – two rooms on top, two on the bottom. Our house is at the end of the lane. Next to our door is an outside toilet.

We get a table, two chairs and two beds from the St Vincent de Paul Society. We're happy. We feel very rich because we can go up and down the stairs all day as much as we want. Dad lights the fire and Mam makes tea. While we're drinking our tea, an old man passes our door with a bucket in his hand. He empties it in our toilet and there's a strong smell in our kitchen. Mam goes to the door.

'Why are you emptying your bucket in our toilet?'

'*Your* toilet, missus? Ah, no. You're making a mistake there, ha, ha. This toilet is for the whole of Roden Lane. Eleven families will be passing your door with their buckets. The smell is very strong in the warm weather, very strong. It's December now, thank God. Good night, missus, I hope you'll be happy in your house.' And he goes back up the road, laughing to himself.

'That's why it's six shillings a week,' says Dad.

***

'I'd like to have a nice Christmas dinner,' says Mam. 'But how can we? They've cut the dole to sixteen shillings since Eugene and Oliver died. Six shillings for the room, ten left. What use is that to four people?'

Dad can't get any work. He gets up early on weekdays and goes to sign for the dole. He always wears a shirt and tie. The bosses always choose him, but when they hear his North of Ireland accent, they take a Limerick man instead.

'Why can't you talk like a Limerick man?' Mam asks him. But he's too proud.

It's December and it's icy cold. Dad wakes me and Malachy when it's light. We go to the toilet in a bucket by the bedroom door. We run downstairs to the fire. We wash under the tap by the front door. The water is so cold that our fingers turn white.

'It's good for you,' says Dad. 'It'll make men of you.'

We have to eat our bread and drink our tea and go to school. Dad tells us to be good boys at school. He says that God is watching every move. 'If you don't do what you're told,' he says, 'you'll go straight to hell and never be cold again.'

One day we come home from school in heavy rain and find the kitchen empty. There are no chairs, no table and no fire. The floor and walls are wet. We go upstairs and find Mam and Dad and the missing furniture. It's nice and warm up there.

'Water came in downstairs,' said Mam. 'There was a terrible smell from people's buckets. We'll stay upstairs while there's rain. Maybe in spring we'll go back down.'

'It's like going away on our holidays,' says Dad. 'To a warm foreign place like Italy. That's what we'll call upstairs from now on – Italy. And downstairs is Ireland.'

Mam takes Malachy and me to the St Vincent de Paul Society. She wants something nice for Christmas and they give us a ticket for some meat.

'You can have a sheep's head or a pig's head with a St Vincent de Paul ticket. That's all, missus,' says the shopkeeper. 'There's plenty of meat on it and the children love it.'

He gets down a pig's head.

'Ooh,' says Malachy, 'it's a dead dog.' Mam and the man laugh. He puts newspaper round it and gives it to Mam and says 'Happy Christmas'. Then he gives her some sausages. 'Have these for breakfast on Christmas Day.'

'Oh, I haven't enough money for sausages.'

'Am I asking you for money? Am I? Take the sausages.'

'You don't have to do that,' says Mam.

'I know that, missus,' he says. 'If I had to do it, I wouldn't.'

I have to carry the pig's head. It feels wet and the newspaper falls away. Boys from school see me and laugh.

'Is that what Yanks eat for Christmas dinner, Frankie?' they shout.

One calls to the other, 'Do you know the only part of the pig the McCourts don't eat?'

'No, I don't.'

'The oink*.'

I feel sorry for the pig. He's dead and the world is

*The noise a pig makes.

laughing at him. My sister and two brothers are dead, too. If anyone laughs at them, I'll hit them with a rock.

Mam's back hurts. She has to stop every few steps and rest. I wish Dad was helping us. But he never carries things, anyway. It's one of his rules.

When we get home, Dad's sitting by the fire. He's reading the *Irish Press* and smoking a cigarette. He looks at me and the pig's head.

'How could you let a boy carry a thing like that through the streets of Limerick?'

She takes off her coat and gets into bed.

'Next Christmas, you find the dinner,' she says.

On Christmas morning, he lights the fire early and we have sausages and bread and tea. Mam puts the pig's head in a big pot, covers it with water and heats it on the fire. Dad takes me and Malachy to church.

When we get home, Mam is in a terrible state. There isn't enough coal to cook the pig's head. We'll have to go down to Dock Road to find some coal. It's no use asking Dad. Mam can't go because of the pain in her back. She sends me and Malachy.

It's a long walk to Dock Road, but we don't mind because our stomachs are full of sausages and it's not raining. We're trying to fill the bag with coal when Pa Keating comes along.

'Jesus, Mary and Joseph,' he says, 'It's Christmas Day and ye don't have a fire for the pig's head. That's a disgrace.'

He takes us to a pub. It shouldn't be open on Christmas Day, but there's a back door for men who want their beer to celebrate the birthday of Jesus. He gets his pint and lemonade for us. He asks the man if he has any coal.

'I've served drink for twenty-seven years but nobody's

ever asked me for coal before.'

He fills our bag because it's Christmas and we pull it home. When Mam sees us, she laughs and then she cries. She laughs because we're black. She cries because we're completely wet. She washes us and puts us to bed.

The room is full of lovely smells when we wake up. But when Dad lifts the pig's head out of the pot, Malachy says, 'Oh, the poor pig. I don't want to eat the poor pig.' Dad cuts off the meat and puts the head under the table. Malachy can eat it now.

***

We have a new brother, Michael. Dad says he found him on the seventh step of the stairs to Italy. He says you have to watch for the Saint of the Seventh Step when you ask for a new baby.

'What do you do if you live in a house with no stairs?' asks Malachy.

'Too many questions, Malachy,' says Dad. 'Too many questions.'

I know that big people don't like questions from children. They can ask all the questions they like: 'How's school?' 'Were you a good boy today?' 'Did you say your prayers?' But if you ask them, 'Did you say your prayers?' you might be hit on the head.

We get a few extra shillings on the dole for Michael, but it's not enough. Mam goes to the St Vincent de Paul Society for food. One night, two men from the Society come to the door.

'Mam and Dad are upstairs in Italy,' I tell them, 'where it's dry.'

They ask about the toilet. 'Why isn't it at the back of the house?'

'It's a good thing it isn't,' I tell them, 'or people would come through our kitchen with buckets all day long.'

'Are you sure there's one toilet for the whole street?' they ask.

'I am.'

'Mother of God,' one says. 'It's a disgrace.'

They step carefully through the lake in the kitchen.

They ask Mam and Dad lots of questions, because big people can ask all the questions they like. They ask about Michael, the dole, Dad's last job and what kind of accent he has. Mam asks if they have any boots for Malachy and me. They say she'll have to ask at the Society.

'Mother of God,' they say on the way out. 'That's not Italy up there, it's Calcutta.'

'You shouldn't beg,' Dad says to Mam when they go.

'Oh, what would you do? Let the boys go around with no shoes?'

'I'd rather mend the shoes they have.'

'You can't mend anything,' says Mam. 'You're useless.'

He comes home the next day with old bits of rubber. He borrows some tools from Mr Hannon next door. When he's finished with the shoes, there are bits of rubber sticking out on all sides. We put the shoes on and I take the tools back.

'What's up with your shoes?' says Mrs Hannon. She laughs, and her husband shakes his head. I don't want to go to school the next day and I pretend to be ill. Dad makes us go. The boys laugh at us. There are six or seven boys with no shoes in my class. I think it's better to have no shoes. Then you have all the no-shoes boys on your side. If you have bits of rubber on your shoes, then it's just you and your brother. You have to fight your own wars. I take off my shoes and hide them in a bucket. When I go into class, Mr Benson wants to know where they are. He knows I'm not a no-shoes boy. I have to get them. Some of the boys laugh when I come back in.

'Are there boys in this room who think they're perfect?' he says to the class. 'Put your hands up.' No hands go up. 'There are boys in this class who have to mend their shoes. There are boys with no shoes. It's not their fault. Our Lord Jesus had no shoes. Was he hanging on the cross with shoes, boys?'

'No, sir.'

'If I hear boys laughing at McCourt or his brother because of their shoes, the stick will come out. What will come out?'

'The stick, sir.'

The boys don't laugh at us after that, and we get new boots a few weeks later from the St Vincent de Paul Society.

***

Dad gets his first job in Limerick at a factory. Friday is payday and Mam cleans the house and sings. We have to wait a long time for him to come home because it's a three-mile walk from the factory. We can't have our tea until he's home and that's very hard because you can smell cooking from the other houses in the street. But he doesn't come home until long after the pubs close. We're all in bed and Mam's crying. We can hear him singing at the top of his voice and people shouting at him to shut up.

'You're not sleeping in this bed tonight,' Mam says to him. He sleeps on a chair in the kitchen, misses work in the morning and loses his job at the factory. We're back on the dole.

# CHAPTER 5
## First Communion

At school Mr Benson says it's time for our First Communion*. We have to learn questions and answers about being a good Catholic. We have to know the difference between right and wrong. And we have to be ready to die for the Church.

It's very useful to have Mikey Molloy living in our street. He's eleven, and he reads books. He already knows everything about girls' bodies and rude things in general.

'The best thing about First Communion,' Mikey tells me, 'is The Collection. Your mother gets you a new suit. She takes you round to all the family and neighbours and they give you money and sweets. Then you can go to the cinema and see James Cagney*.'

Mikey got five shillings on his First Communion Day and ate so many sweets that he was sick in the cinema. He wants to go to the cinema for the rest of his life, sit next to girls from our street and do rude things. When he's older he'll go to the pub like his father and drink beer all night.

'I'll tell you more when you grow up, Frankie. You're too young now and you don't know your arse from your elbow*.'

***

Our teacher Mr Benson is very old. He gets very angry when he's trying to prepare us for First Communion. We have to learn everything in Irish and English. If we forget an Irish word he gets his stick out. He tells us we're a disgrace to Ireland and her long, sad history. He says

*People take communion in church. The priest gives them a wafer to eat and wine to drink.
*James Cagney was a famous Hollywood actor of the 1930s and 40s.
*Mikey means that Frankie doesn't know anything.

we're the worst class he's ever had for First Communion. He says he'll hit us until we're good Catholics.

'There are boys in this class,' he shouts, 'who will never know the love of Our Lord. And why? Because they are greedy. I have heard them in the school playground talking about First Communion, the happiest day of your life. Are they talking about receiving the body and blood of Our Lord? Oh no! Those greedy little beggars are talking about the money they'll get.' He says that if he hears another boy in this class talk about The Collection, he'll hit him until his blood pours out.

He shows us how to receive Holy Communion in the classroom. We get down on our knees by our desks. We have to stick out our tongue and he places a bit of newspaper on it. Then we pull in our tongue, put our hands together in prayer and look up to heaven.

'Make sure you put your tongue out correctly,' he says. 'The worst thing for a priest is if you let the Communion wafer* fall to the floor. The priest has to pick it up with his tongue. He could get an illness from the floor and die.'

Before we receive First Communion, we have to tell the priest all our sins. Mr Benson tells us what to say. 'I told a lie. I hit my brother. I stole a penny from my mother's purse. I ate a sausage on a Friday*.' We've all got the same sins to tell the priest.

But then I get a sin that no one else has. Mikey Molloy tells me a rude story about women. Then he says it's a sin to listen to a story with a bad word in it.

Now I don't know what to do. How can I tell the priest this terrible thing before my First Communion? The priest will say I'm a disgrace and throw me into the street. Everyone will know I listened to a story about women

*The Communion wafer represents the body of Christ.
*Catholics are not allowed to eat meat on Fridays.

with a bad word in it. Mothers will tell their little children, 'Look at him. He never made his First Communion. He walks around in a state of sin, he never made The Collection and he never saw James Cagney.'

The day before First Communion, Mr Benson takes us to the church to tell the priest our sins. If we say a single word on the way, he'll kill us in the street and send us to hell full of sin. We whisper about our big sins. Willie Harrold saw his sister with no clothes on. Paddy Hartigan stole ten shillings from his aunt's purse and made himself sick with ice-cream and chips. Brendan Quigley ran away from home and spent half the night in a wood with four sheep. I try to tell them about Mikey and the rude story but Mr Benson sees me talking. He hits me on the head.

We wait in the church. Then it's my turn. The priest's box is dark and there's a big cross over my head. The priest opens the little wooden door. 'Yes, my child?'

I tell him my sins about the lie and my brother and the penny. 'Yes, my child. Anything else?'

'I ... I listened to a story.'

'That's not a sin, my child.'

I tell him the story. He has his hand over his mouth and is making strange sounds. When he can speak again, he tells me to say a special prayer for him.

'I will, Father. Was that the worst sin? Am I the worst of all boys?'

'No, my child. You have a long way to go.'

That night I couldn't sleep. I thought about The Collection and James Cagney.

We slept late. Grandma came in the morning and woke us up. She and Mam washed me until my skin was red and sore all over. They dressed me in my black First Communion suit. My mother had saved for a year to buy the suit. We had to run to the church. The last boy had just taken Communion when we got there. The priest looked hard at me. He placed the Communion wafer on my tongue. The body and blood of Jesus. At last.

I wanted to go and make The Collection but Grandma said no. Before that, I had to have a First Communion breakfast at her house.

I ate the egg. I ate the sausage. I felt ill. I ran into her back garden. Back came the egg and the sausage.

'Look at what he did!,' screamed Grandma. 'He's been sick. There's the body and blood of Jesus all over my back garden. What I am going to do?' She told all the neighbours about God in her back garden.

'Ye can forget about The Collection and the cinema,' she said to me. 'Ye're not a real Catholic. Now go home.'

'Wait a minute,' said Mam. 'That's my son on his First Communion Day. He's going to see James Cagney.'

It was a brilliant film but sad. They shot James Cagney and his poor old Irish mother was very upset.

James Cagney in 'Public Enemy'

# CHAPTER 6
## Dancing lessons

Grandma hears about a man looking for a room. His name is Bill Galvin and he has a good job at the factory. She gives him her bed and moves into the small room with Uncle Pat, Mam's brother. Uncle Pat was dropped on his head when he was a baby and he always does what Grandma tells him.

Every morning, Grandma cooks Bill's dinner and takes it to the factory.

'School's finished,' Mam tells her. 'Give Frankie sixpence a week and he'll take Bill's dinner.'

'Take the dinner straight there,' Grandma tells me.

There's a lovely smell from the dinner can. There's meat and vegetables and two big white potatoes. He won't notice if I try half a potato. He never speaks much, so he won't say anything to Grandma.

I'd better eat the other half or he'll wonder why he got a half. I'll just try the meat and the vegetables. And if I eat the other potato, he'll just think she didn't send one at all.

The second potato tastes wonderful and I'll have to try another bit of vegetable, another little piece of meat. There isn't much left now. I'll finish it.

What am I going to do now? Grandma will destroy me. Mam will keep me in for a year. Bill Galvin will kill me. I'll tell him a dog attacked me and ate the whole dinner.

'Oh, is that so?' says Bill Galvin. 'And what's that bit of meat at the corner of your mouth? Go home and tell your grandmother you ate my whole dinner and I'm falling down dead with hunger here.'

'She'll kill me.'

'If you don't go, I'll kill you and throw you in the river.'

So I tell Grandma, 'He wants more dinner.'

'Jesus above,' she says, 'does he have a hole in his leg? I will not send him more dinner.'

'He didn't get his dinner.'

'He didn't? Why not?'

'I ate it.'

'What?'

'I was hungry. I tasted it and I couldn't stop.'

'Jesus, Mary and Joseph.' She hits me so hard it brings tears to my eyes. She screams at me. She points her knife at me when she cuts bread and makes Bill Galvin sandwiches. She'll take me to the priest, the bishop and the pope, she says.

She runs to Mam. For my terrible sin, I have to take Bill Galvin's dinner for a fortnight with no pay. I have to sit and watch him eat it and take the empty can back to Grandma. Then she makes me say a prayer to the Sacred Heart of Jesus.

***

Mam and Dad have terrible teeth. They're all brown and black. Dad says the holes in his teeth are big enough for a bird to lay its eggs in. They tell us it's the smoking.

'If I ever catch you with a cigarette in your mouth,' says Mam, 'I'll break your face.'

One day they get their old teeth pulled out and they get new teeth. Dad shows us his big new white smile and he looks like an American. When he tells us a ghost story, he pushes his bottom teeth up to his nose and frightens us. Mam says she'll stop smoking now, but she never does. The new teeth hurt and the smoking helps with the pain.

Every night they leave their teeth in the kitchen in glasses of water. Malachy whispers to me in the middle of the night, 'Do you want to go downstairs to Ireland and see if we can wear the teeth?'

The teeth are big. Malachy pushes Dad's teeth in and can't get them out again. His mouth is stuck in a mad smile. I laugh but soon there are tears in his eyes. Dad calls down, 'What are you boys doing?' Malachy runs upstairs to Italy and I hear Mam and Dad laughing, until they realise that Malachy might die.

Dad and I run to the hospital with Malachy. The doctor pours oil in Malachy's mouth and gets the teeth out in a second. Then he looks at me and says to Dad, 'Why is that child's mouth hanging open?'

'He always looks like that.'

The doctor looks up my nose, in my ears, down my throat and feels my neck.

'The tonsils,' he says. 'They have to come out. The sooner the better or he'll look stupid all his life with his mouth wide open.'

The next day, Malachy gets sweets for sticking teeth in his mouth. I have to have my tonsils out.

***

One day Mam says, 'You're going to dancing classes.'

'Dancing? Why?'

'You're seven years old and it's time for dancing. I'm taking you to Mrs O'Connor's Irish dancing classes. It'll keep you off the streets every Saturday morning.'

She tells me about Cyril Benson. 'He wins cups and gets his name in the newspapers. I'm sure he wins lots of money and he looks lovely in his dancing skirt.'

If my friends see me going to an Irish dancing class, I'll be a disgrace forever. We all like Fred Astaire and Ginger Rogers* at the cinema, but there's nothing like that in Irish

*Fred Astaire and Ginger Rogers were famous dancers in Hollywood films in the 1930s.

dancing. You stand up straight, keep your arms by your sides, kick your legs up and around, and never smile. Uncle Pa Keating says Irish dancers look like they have metal rulers up their arses. I can't say that to Mam, she'd kill me.

Mrs O'Connor is a big fat woman. I don't know how she can teach dancing. Mam gives her sixpence and I stand in line with the other boys and girls. I don't want to be here.

'Now look at Cyril,' says Mrs O'Connor. 'There he goes, and I taught him every step he knows. He dances like he's come down from heaven. What's that strange look you have, Frankie McCourt? Pick up your feet, one-two-three, one-two-three. Oh, Maura, will you help Frankie before he ties his feet together?'

Maura is a big girl of about ten. She pulls me round the room until I feel sick. I look completely stupid and go bright red.

'What did you learn?' asks Mam when I get home. She makes me dance round the kitchen, one-two-three, one-two-three, and has a good laugh.

'That's not bad for your first time. You'll be as good as Cyril Benson in a month.'

On the fourth Saturday Billy Campbell knocks at our door. 'Can Frankie come out and play?'

'No, Billy,' Mam says. 'Frankie's going dancing.'

He waits for me on the way.

'Why are you dancing? Dancing is for girls. Next you'll be in the kitchen making cakes. You'll forget how to play football or anything.'

I tell Billy I'm finished with dancing. I have sixpence in my pocket and I'm going to the cinema. I can pay for both of us with sixpence and we can get sweets too.

When I get home, Mam and Dad say, 'What did you learn today?' I make up a dance. Dad says, 'Oh, you'll make a fine Irish dancer.' Mam says, 'That wasn't much for sixpence.'

A few weeks later, they're waiting for me but they're not smiling. Some boy from the dancing class saw me go into the cinema. He told Mrs O'Connor and she sent a note home. 'Is Frankie all right?' she asked. 'He will be able to dance just like Cyril Benson one day. But I haven't seen him for ages.' Dad takes me to the priest.

The priest tells me I'm bad for going to the cinema, although he thinks dancing is almost as sinful as films. I sinned by taking my mother's sixpence and lying. 'You're dancing at the gates of hell, child,' he says.

***

I'm nearly ten and Dad is still on the dole. If he gets a job, he loses it in the third week.

'Why can't he be like the other men in the lanes?' Mam asks her friend Bridey Hannon from next door. 'They're home before six and give their pay to the wife. They change their shirt, have their tea, get a few shillings back from the wife and go to the pub for a pint or two. He buys pints for all the other men in the pub with the dole money while his children are at home with empty stomachs. Oh Bridey, I don't know what I'm going to do.'

Bridey smokes her cigarette, drinks her tea and says God is good.

'I'm sure God is good,' says Mam, 'but He hasn't been seen lately in the lanes of Limerick.'

Bridey laughs. 'Angela, you could go to hell for that.'

'Aren't I there already, Bridey?'

***

Dad says it's time for me to be an altar boy*. He was an altar boy when he was ten. I get down on my knees on the kitchen floor. He teaches me the whole Mass in Latin.

'Let him sit on a chair,' says Mam.

'Latin has to be learned on the knees,' says Dad. 'You won't find the pope sitting around drinking tea while he speaks Latin.'

After a fortnight I've learned the Mass. I'd like to be an altar boy and wear the red and white clothes. I'd like to answer the priest in Latin, move the big book, pour water and wine into the cup, pour water over the priest's hands, with everyone in the church looking at me.

Mam and Dad spend an hour washing me. 'You can be proud of your family,' Mam says. 'You come from good blood, McCourts and Sheehans. And Grandma's family, the Guilfoyles, who owned land in County Limerick before the English stole it.'

Dad takes me to St Joseph's Church. We ask for Stephen Carey, who chooses the altar boys.

'This is my son Frank,' Dad says. 'He knows Latin and is ready to be an altar boy.'

Stephen Carey looks at him, then me. He says, 'We don't have room for him,' and closes the door.

Dad holds my hand so tight it hurts. He says nothing on the way home.

'They don't want boys from the lanes on the altar,' says Mam when we get home. 'They want nice boys with new shoes. It's hard to keep your religion when it's one rule for the rich and another for the poor.'

*An altar boy helps the priest during the Mass; the Mass is the main service in the Roman Catholic Church; Latin was the language of the Roman Empire and the language of the Roman Catholic Church.

# CHAPTER 7
# Mr O'Neill's apple

I'm in the fourth class at school and Mr O'Neill is the teacher. He is a fan of Euclid*. 'Without Euclid, boys,' he says, 'the bicycle would have no wheel. Without Euclid, we would not have maths.'

Paddy Clohessy whispers behind me, 'I hate Euclid.'

'What, Clohessy,' shouts Mr O'Neill, 'were you saying to McCourt?'

'I said we should get down on our two knees and thank God for Euclid.'

'I'm sure you did, Clohessy. I see the lie at the corners of your mouth.'

Every day Mr O'Neill brings an apple to school. He sits at his desk and cuts the skin off slowly in one long piece. He looks around the room with a little smile. He asks us questions like, 'Who is the President of the United States?' If you're the first boy to answer his questions, he gives you the skin. Some days the questions are too hard and he throws it away.

Today he asks, 'Who stood at the foot of the cross when Our Lord was hanging on the cross?'

Fintan Slattery puts his hand up. Of course Fintan knows. He and his mother spend all their time on their knees in church. His mother is so saintly his father ran off to Canada to cut down trees. They read religious magazines every evening. They go to Communion and Mass if it's wet or sunny. If you push Fintan in the playground, he says he'll pray for you. His sister ran away to England when she was seventeen, and we all know he wears her blouse at home.

*Euclid was a Greek mathematician in the third century BC.

Of course he knows who was at the foot of the cross. He probably knows what they were wearing and what they had for breakfast. 'It was the three Marys*,' he says.

Fintan gets his apple skin. He takes out a pocketknife and cuts it into pieces.

'I'd like to give pieces of my apple,' he says, 'to Quigley, Clohessy and McCourt.'

'Why, Fintan?'

'They're my friends, sir.'

The boys around the room are laughing behind their hands. The playground will be hell now. What will I say? If Paddy Clohessy says thanks, I'll say thanks. He says, 'Thanks very much, Fintan,' eats the apple skin and goes red. I do too, and all the boys laugh again and I want to hit them.

After school, a big boy says to Paddy, 'Are you wearing your sister's blouse tonight then?'

'Shut up,' says Paddy.

'Oh, and who's going to make me shut up?' the boy says. Paddy tries to hit him but the big boy hits his nose and there's blood. I try to kick the big boy. He picks me up and hits my head against the wall until I can see lights.

***

A few days later Fintan asks me and Paddy back to his flat at lunchtime. His mother won't be there and she leaves his lunch for him. He might give us some too and he has lovely milk, he says.

'Will it be better than the school bread and milk?' I ask.

'It will,' says Paddy.

Fintan's flat is like a church. The Sacred Heart of Jesus is on the wall and there's a picture of St Francis of Assisi. He

*The Virgin Mary and Mary Magdalene are two of the three Marys.

tells us to sit at the table in the kitchen. We can read his comic books if we like. Fintan sits in front of his sandwich and glass of milk.

'Is that a cheese sandwich?' asks Paddy.

'It is,' says Fintan.

Fintan carefully cuts the sandwich into small pieces. He reads a magazine while he eats his sandwich and drinks his milk. Paddy and I watch him and wonder why we're here. He finishes his meal, thanks God for it and says we'll be late for afternoon school.

It's too late for me and Paddy to get the lunchtime bread and milk at school. Paddy stops at the school gate.

'I can't go in there dying of hunger,' he says. 'I'll fall asleep and O'Neill will kill me.'

'Come on,' says Fintan, 'we'll be late.'

'You had your lunch. We had nothing,' Paddy shouts at Fintan. 'You're a little beggar with your sandwich and your Sacred Heart of Jesus on the wall. You can kiss my arse. Come on, Frankie.'

Paddy and I walk until we get to a farm. We climb a wall into a field of apple trees. We eat apples until we're

full and then we stick our faces into a lovely, cool river to drink. Then there's a shout and a man with a stick is running across the field. We're over the wall in a minute and he can't follow us because of his big rubber boots.

But I don't want to rob apple fields forever. I want to win O'Neill's apple skin. Then I can go home and tell Dad I answered the hard questions.

We walk back. It starts to rain really hard and we get wet through. Quigley rides towards us on a big woman's bicycle.

'Oi, Frankie McCourt. You're going to be killed. O'Neill sent a note to your house. He said you bunked off* with Paddy Clohessy.'

Oh God. I feel cold and empty. I wish I was in India where it's nice and warm and my father couldn't find me.

Quigley laughs and rides off. I don't know why he's laughing – he once spent the night in a wood with four sheep and that's worse.

'Don't worry, Frankie,' says Paddy. 'They're always sending notes to our house and we put them on the fire.'

But I'm afraid to go home.

'Come on,' says Paddy, 'we'll go down to Dock Road and throw stones in the River Shannon.'

We throw stones in the river and it's getting dark. I don't know where I'm going to sleep. Paddy says I can go home with him. I can sleep on the floor and dry out.

Paddy lives in a tall house by the river. Everyone in Limerick knows these houses might fall down at any minute. Mam says the people are wild down here.

Small children are playing on the stairs. Some of the stairs are missing. There's thick dirt on the ones that aren't missing.

*Stayed away from school and didn't tell anyone.

Paddy's family live in one big room on the fourth floor. His father is in a bed in the corner. He has consumption and he coughs blood and green stuff into a bucket. Paddy's brothers and sisters are on beds on the floor. There's a baby with no clothes on getting closer to Paddy's father's bucket. Paddy pulls him away.

His mother comes in. 'Jesus,' she says, 'those stairs will kill me.' She finds some bread and makes tea.

Paddy's father asks who I am, who my father is and who my mother is.

'Angela Sheehan!' he says. 'Ah, Frankie,' and he coughs wildly, 'I knew your mother well. I danced with her and a wonderful dancer she was too.'

He coughs more stuff into the bucket but he doesn't stop talking. He makes me dance round the room so that he can remember his young days with Angela at the dancehall. He laughs and coughs and I feel sick looking at the stuff going in the bucket. Should I go home and let my parents kill me if they want to?

Paddy lies down under the window and I lie beside him. I keep my clothes on like everybody else, even though they're wet. Paddy falls asleep at once. I lie awake.

It's my first time away from my family and I know I'd rather be in my own house with the smelly toilet next door. I'd rather be in a wood with four sheep.

In the morning there's a knock at the door and it's Mam with my little brother, Michael. Michael runs to me.

'Mammy was crying for you, Frankie,' he says.

'Where were you all night? Your father looked for you along every street in Limerick,' says Mam.

'Who's at the door?' says Mr Clohessy. 'God above, is that Angela? Angela, it's me, Dennis Clohessy.'

'Ah, no,' says Mam.

'It is. I know I'm changed. The consumption is killing me. Remember the nights at the dancehall, Angela, and the fish and chips after?'

My mother has tears running down her face. 'You were a great dancer, Dennis Clohessy.'

'We could have won cups, Angela. But you had to run off to America.'

Mam takes us back to school. She cries all the way. Michael says, 'Don't cry, Mammy. Frankie won't run away.'

'I'm not crying about Frankie. It's the nights at the dancehall and the fish and chips after.'

She comes into school with us. O'Neill looks very cross. He tells me and Paddy to sit down and wait for him. He talks a long time at the door with my mother. When she leaves, he doesn't say anything to us. He puts his hand on Paddy's head as he walks to the front of the class.

I'm sorry for the Clohessys and all their troubles. But I think they saved me from trouble with my teacher and my mother that day.

# CHAPTER 8
# Confirmation

One day Mam moves her bed down to Ireland. She can't climb the stairs to Italy, she says. School is over and we can stay in bed in the mornings if we like.

Then one day in July, Dad says we can't go downstairs. He stands at the door. We push our bedclothes up in the air and pretend we're in a tent.

Then there's a cry from downstairs and Malachy says, 'Dad, did Mam get a new baby?'

'Oh yes, son,' says Dad. 'Another boy.'

Grandpa McCourt in the North sends five pounds for our new baby, Alphie. Mam can't go far from her bed so Dad says he'll collect it from the post office. She sends me and Malachy with him.

He gets the money and says to us, 'All right, boys, go home and tell your mother I'll be home in a few minutes.'

Malachy says, 'Dad, you're not to go to the pub. You're not to drink beer.'

I say, 'Give us the money. The money is for the baby.'

'Francis, don't be a bad boy. Do what your father says.'

He walks away from us and into the nearest pub.

Mam is sitting by the fire with Alphie in her arms. 'He went to the pub, didn't he?' It's bad enough to drink the dole or your pay, but to drink the baby's money is the worst.

***

I'm ten years old and ready for my Confirmation. The priests tell us that Confirmation means you can fight and die for the Church. More dying. I want to tell them I've already promised to die for Ireland. Does anyone in the world want us to live?

We have Confirmation Day and The Collection. That's where Peter Dooley comes in. We call him Quasimodo because he has a back like the Hunchback of Notre Dame*. Quasimodo has nine sisters. He's fifteen and his red hair sticks up. His right leg isn't straight and when he walks he does a little dance. Before he leaves his house, he always sticks his head out of the door and says, 'Here's my head, my arse is coming.' And then you're surprised because he has a beautiful English accent that he learned from the radio. He wants to work for the BBC in London. But he needs money to get to London.

Quasimodo knows it's our Confirmation and he has an idea for Billy and me. If we promise to pay him a shilling, we can look at his sisters' bodies. They take their weekly wash on a Friday. Billy says, 'I have my own sister. Why should I pay to look at yours?'

'Looking at your own sister's body is the worst sin of all. No priest would forgive you. You'd have to go to the bishop, and think of the disgrace.'

On Friday night, we climb the wall behind Quasimodo's house. Mikey Molloy comes too and he's fourteen so he goes first. He climbs onto the toilet roof and then onto the next bit of roof so he's outside the sisters' window. Suddenly he starts to fall. He screams as he lands on the ground. Quasimodo's mother runs out of the kitchen. The sisters are screaming from the window above. She pushes us all into the kitchen. She kicks Quasimodo into the hall and locks him in the coal hole.

Our mothers are there in no time. Mam pulls me home by the ear.

'Did you look at Mona Dooley's body with nothing on?'

'I did not.'

*Quasimodo is the hero of a novel by French writer Victor Hugo, *The Hunchback of Notre Dame* (1831).

'If you're lying, God will know at your Confirmation tomorrow. Only the bishop could forgive a sin like that. Do you hear?'

'I do.'

'Go to bed and stay away from that Quasimodo Dooley.'

Six months later Quasimodo died of consumption, and he never went to London.

We are all confirmed the next day.

I forget all about Quasimodo because my nose starts bleeding and I feel sick. Confirmation boys and girls are outside St Joseph's with their parents and I don't care. My father is working and I don't care. The boys talk about The Collection and I don't care. I want to lie down. Mam says, Grandma is making me a nice breakfast. I think of food and run to the edge of the road to be sick.

Mam takes me home and puts me to bed. She brings tea but I'm sick into the bucket. Mrs Hannon comes in from next door. 'That child needs a doctor,' she says.

'It's Saturday. Where would you get a doctor?' Dad and Grandma say it's my age, it's growing pains.

The next day I'm very hot and there's blood all over the bed. Dr Troy is on holiday. A different doctor comes and he smells of whisky. He tells my mother I have a bad cold. Days pass and I sleep. There's more blood. Mrs Hannon comes again. 'That doctor doesn't know what he's talking about,' she says. 'See if Dr Troy is back.'

Dr Troy comes. He feels my head, looks in my eyes, looks at my back, picks me up and runs to his motor car.

'He has typhoid fever, Mrs McCourt.'

'Oh God, oh God, am I to lose my whole family? Will it ever end?' She gets in the car and cries all the way to the hospital.

I nearly die, but I don't. After fourteen weeks in the

hospital, they tell me I can go home. The doctor says I need good food and rest.

I lie in bed in Roden Lane with the fleas and think of the hospital. The white sheets were changed every day and there wasn't a single flea. There was a bathroom where you could sit on the toilet and read your book all day. There was a bath where you could sit in hot water as long as you liked.

In November I go back to school and they put me back into fifth class because I've missed so much.

'I don't want to be in fifth class, Mam. Malachy is in that class. I made my Confirmation last year. I'm not bigger than them because of the typhoid, but I'm older.'

'It won't kill you,' says Mam.

All Malachy's friends are laughing at me and Mr O'Dea makes me sit in the front. 'And get that strange look off your face,' he says, 'or I'll get it off with my stick.'

Then St Francis helps me. I find a penny in the street. I want to get some chocolate but I also want to get out of fifth class. I go to the church and pray to St Francis. I put my penny in his box. 'Get me out of fifth class,' I beg him. St Francis doesn't say a word but I know he's listening. What's the use of being named after someone who doesn't listen?

Mr O'Dea gives me some writing for homework. The title is, 'What would it be like if Our Lord Jesus had lived in Limerick?' The next day I have to read it to the class. I call it 'Jesus and the Weather'. After I've read it, Mr O'Dea takes me to Mr O'Halloran's room and shows him my writing.

'Did your father write this, McCourt?'

'He didn't, sir.'

I'm taken out of fifth class and put into Mr O'Halloran's

class with all the boys I know.

After school, I go back to thank St Francis.

Was it something good I said in the homework or something bad? I don't know.

Mr O'Halloran teaches sixth, seventh and eighth class in one room. He carries a long stick and if you give stupid answers or don't pay attention, he hits you three times on each hand. He loves America and we learn all the American states starting with A for Alabama. We learn the Irish language, Irish history and maths. He tells us what is important and why. No other teacher has ever done that. He doesn't call us stupid. If we ask a question, he doesn't shout and scream. He tells us about the Irish fighting the English. He tells us the Irish were no better or worse than the English. We can't believe it! All these years, the teachers have told us the Irish fought well and bravely before the English killed them.

'You have to study and learn so that you can decide for yourself about history and everything else,' he tell us. 'But you must have facts. You might be poor, your shoes might be broken, but your head is a palace.'

***

My father is like three people in one. There's the one in the morning. He lights the fire and makes the tea and reads the paper to me in a whisper. He tells me about the world, about Hitler, Mussolini and Franco. He says the war is not our business – the English are making trouble as usual. He tells me about the great President Roosevelt in Washington. 'You must be good in school, Frankie,' he says. 'One day you'll go back to America and have a job in an office. You'll sit at a desk with two pens in your pocket, one red and one blue, and you'll tell people what to do.

You can do anything in America. It's not a grey, wet place like Limerick.'

Then there's the one at night. He helps us with our homework. He makes up wild adventure stories about people who live in our lane. He says our prayers with us. We thank God for Mam, our dead brothers and sister, Ireland and anyone who gives Dad a job.

And then there's the bad one. He comes home smelling of whisky and wants us to die for Ireland.

If I were in America, I could say, 'I love you, Dad,' like they do in the films. But you can't say that in Limerick or people would laugh at you.

# CHAPTER 9
# The man of the house

The English want Irishmen to work in the factories while all the Englishmen are fighting Hitler. The money is good and there are no jobs in Limerick. Families with fathers in England run to the post office on Saturdays for their money. The new rich people get haircuts and eat meat, potatoes, sweets and cakes on Sundays. They have tea in town and have electricity in their houses. They thank God for Hitler. He got the men of Ireland off their arses, they say.

Dad says he'll never help the English win a war. Mam says, 'If I had the money for the boat ticket, I'd go to England myself. I'm sure they need women to work.'

Dad says, 'A factory is no place for a woman.'

Mam says, 'Sitting on your arse by the fire is no place for a man.'

I say to him, 'Why don't you go to England, Dad? Then we can have electricity and a radio.'

When America joins the war against Hitler, he agrees to go. He thinks there must be some good in it if the Americans are in it. 'You're the man of the house now, Frankie,' he tells me.

He goes to Coventry* with Mr Meehan from the top of our lane. After he goes, Mam says, 'Surely our troubles will be over now. Surely.'

On Saturdays, the telegram boys ride through the lanes on their bicycles. They bring the money from the men in England. When the telegram boy stops at the Meehans, we know we're next. Mam has her coat on ready to go to the

*Coventry is an industrial city in the middle of England where factories produced things needed in World War II.

post office. He goes to another house with a telegram and then he turns his bicycle around before he gets to us. 'Telegram boy!' calls Malachy. 'Do you have something for McCourt? Our first one is coming today. It should be three pounds or more.' The boy shakes his head and rides away. Michael asks if we're having fish and chips tonight.

'Next week, love,' says Mam, and she turns the dead ashes in the fire.

Something happens to my eyes. They're red and sore and there's sticky yellow stuff coming out of them. When I wake up in the morning, they're stuck together. They don't get better. Grandma says it's because I read too many books.

We go to Dr Troy. He sends me to the eye hospital.

The eye doctor pours some brown stuff into my right eye and it feels like my head's on fire.

I spend a month in the eye hospital. Then the doctor says I can go home. 'The eyes are nearly better. Keep them clean with soap and clean towels,' he tells Mam. 'Make the boy strong with plenty of meat and eggs, and he'll have shiny new eyes in no time.' Meat and eggs! Ha ha.

***

Old Mrs Downes across the street dies. Her son comes back from England. He tells Bridey about my father and Bridey tells Mam. 'Your Malachy has gone mad with the drink. He spends all his money in pubs all over Coventry. Mr Downes says he's a disgrace.'

Mam is ill. She's hot and cold and calling for lemonade. My brothers are dying of hunger. Kathleen at the shop doesn't want to give us any more food unless we can pay for it. She's already been very kind. Everyone knows the telegram isn't coming. I'll have to ask Kathleen for food anyway. I'll tell her my mother is sick in bed.

It's February and it's cold in the streets. There's a lorry leaving from outside the pub. There are boxes of beer and lemonade on the street and there's nobody about. In a second I have two bottles of lemonade under my shirt. The bread van is outside Kathleen's shop. I know it's wrong to steal from Kathleen. She's always good to us. I promise to tell the priest.

The boys tear the bread and Mam drinks the lemonade. We sit round the fire and I tell my brothers about stealing the bread and lemonade. Michael is worried they'll put me in prison but Malachy says it's only like Robin Hood*. He stole from the rich to give to the poor and everyone thinks he was a great man.

The next morning it's just getting light and I start thinking about food. Mam is still asleep but her face is red and she's making strange sounds. I have to be careful in the streets that Guard Dennehy doesn't see me. Guard Dennehy goes round on his bicycle and catches boys who are bunking off. He pulls them to school by the ear.

I go to the roads where the rich houses are. I see a box outside one. I pretend to knock on the door so I can look in the box. There's a bottle of milk, a loaf of bread, fruit and, oh God, cheese. I can't get all that under my shirt. Shall I take the whole box? People in the street don't pay me any attention. I lift the whole box and try to look like a shop boy. No one says a word.

Malachy and Michael go mad when they see inside the box. I give Mam the rest of the lemonade from yesterday. We're having a fine time until Mam starts shouting about her lovely daughter and her two dead boys.

'Will Mam die?' asks Michael.

'You can't die until a priest comes,' says Malachy.

*Robin Hood and his band of men lived in Sherwood Forest. They robbed the rich and gave to the poor.

We're really cold and we have no coal.

'Why don't we go and ask at the rich houses for coal?' says Malachy. 'We'll take Alphie.'

We push Alphie up to the big houses. We knock on the doors. Girls answer the door and tell us to go away. 'You're a disgrace,' they say. 'That baby should be at home in the warm.' So Malachy and I take Alphie round the back of the houses. Michael knocks at the front door. Malachy and I climb over the wall at the back and throw the coal to Alphie. But then a piece of coal hits Alphie on the head and he cries loudly and we have to run home.

Later, Guard Dennehy is at the door.

'Hello, hello. Are you there, Mrs McCourt?'

I call out of the window, 'I can't open the door. My mother is ill. It may be typhoid fever. It could kill you.'

He pushes open the door and climbs up to Italy. Alphie comes out from under the bed at that moment. He's covered in dirt.

'Jesus, Mary and Joseph,' he says. 'This is a terrible situation.' He sends me to get Grandma and Aunt Aggie. They scream at me and tell me I'm dirty and a disgrace. They push me back to Roden Lane.

'Mother of God, Angela,' says Grandma. 'What's up with you?'

'She wants lemonade,' says Michael. 'We got it for her and bread and cheese. We're all like Robin Hood now.'

Dr Troy comes in his car and he takes my mother to hospital. We all want to go in the car but we have to go to Aunt Aggie's.

'Get your clothes,' she says to us. She finds an old shirt to tie round Alphie's bottom. We're still standing there. 'Get your clothes!' she says again.

'They're on us,' I say. She shakes her head.

I don't know why Aunt Aggie is always angry with us. She has electric light in the house and her own outside toilet. Uncle Pa has a good job and brings the money home every Friday. What more does she want?

We have good times with Uncle Pa when Aunt Aggie goes out to play cards. He buys two bottles of beer and bread and meat. We sit by the fire and eat sandwiches and drink tea. He tells us about the world and makes us laugh.

There are days when Aunt Aggie won't have us in the house for another minute. 'Do anything you like,' she says, 'but don't come back before teatime.' It's cold but we don't care. We push Alphie out into the country and we let him run about in the field with the cows and sheep. We laugh when the cows smell Alphie. We laugh when the farmer chases us. We're late back but we don't care. Aggie can shout at us but we had a fine time and you can tell she never has fine times.

The next day Michael runs in from the street.

'Dad's here, Dad's here,' he shouts. Soon we're back in our house in Roden Lane. Mam comes home. She's weak and white and walks slowly. Dad makes tea and fries bread on the fire. We have a lovely night up in Italy where it's warm.

Dad goes back to Coventry. In a week there's a letter from him. He tells us to be good boys, say our prayers and be good to our mother. A week later there's a telegram for three pounds and we're in heaven. We'll be rich, there'll be fish and chips, films every Saturday at the cinema and tea at the Savoy Café in Limerick.

The next Saturday there's no telegram, nor the one after that, nor any Saturday. Mam begs at the St Vincent de Paul. She spends most of her time by the fire with Bridey, smoking and drinking tea. She never washes the cups or cleans the table, and there are flies in the sugar.

# CHAPTER 10
## A working man

Mr Hannon from next door, Bridey's father, is a coal man. He takes coal to houses all over Limerick. He's having terrible trouble with his legs. He has to climb up and down all day to get the bags of coal. The doctor tells him to stay off his legs.

'How can he work if he stays off his legs?' says Mrs Hannon. 'What would you think, Mrs McCourt,' she continues, 'if your boy Frankie went round with John for a few hours a week and helped him with the bags? We could pay him a shilling or two and John could rest his poor legs.'

'I don't know,' says Mam. 'He's only eleven and the coal would be bad for his sore eyes and he had typhoid fever.'

On Saturday morning down at Dock Road, Mr Hannon and I get the horse ready. Mr Hannon has a lovely way with the horse. The bag men put the bags of coal up behind the horse and we drive off. When the rain starts, we cover ourselves with empty bags. We stop at the first house. Mr Hannon climbs down and I push the first bag of coal onto his shoulders.

The sun comes out when we reach the last house and the horse knows his work day is over. It's lovely sitting up there behind the horse.

'Go to school, Frankie,' Mr Hannon tells me. 'Don't be like me. Get out of Limerick and Ireland itself. The world is wide and you can have great adventures.'

Mr Hannon buys me a lemonade and gives me a shilling for my morning's work. He says I'm a great worker and I can help him after school next week. I'm so happy I want to jump up and down. I see myself in a window on the way home. I'm all black from the coal, I have a shilling in my pocket and I feel like a man.

I work with Mr Hannon on Tuesdays and Thursdays after school and a half day on Saturday. That means three shillings for my mother, though she worries all the time about my sore eyes. The minute I get home she washes them and I have to rest for half an hour. On Thursdays Mr Hannon waits for me outside school. The boys from school see me and they can't believe it. I'm in heaven because Mr Hannon lets me drive the horse.

They don't call me names now. Big boys of thirteen stick their faces in mine. They say they should have that job because I'm only eleven with no shoulders. I don't care because I have the job and they don't.

Mr Hannon's sore legs get worse. He can only just walk. My sore eyes get worse. I can only just see. The doctor sends Mr Hannon to hospital. His working days are over and my big job is gone.

'Frank,' Mrs Hannon tells me, 'you made Mr Hannon very happy going round with him. Did you know that?'

'I didn't.'

'We had two daughters, Bridey that you know, and Kathleen who's a nurse in Dublin. But no son. And he felt you were like a son.'

My eyes are burning but I don't want her to see me cry.

'I won't have a job now, Mrs Hannon.'

'You have a job, Frank. School. You'll never have another job like it. You and the coal – it breaks Mr Hannon's heart and your mother's heart and it will destroy your eyes.'

'Can I visit Mr Hannon?'

'You can, Frank. God knows he won't have much to do except read and look out of the window.'

***

Dad's coming home for Christmas. Everything will be different, says his letter, he's a new man and he's bringing us all something for Christmas.

When he walks in the door, his two front teeth are missing and he's got a black eye. He says the sea was rough coming over from England.

'It wouldn't be a fight, would it?' says Mam. 'It wouldn't be the drink?'

'Oh no, Angela.'

'What have you brought us, Dad?' asks Michael.

He takes a box of chocolates from his suitcase and gives it to Mam. She opens it and shows us the inside. Half the chocolates are gone.

'Are you sure you don't want to finish them?' she says to him. And she puts the box away for Christmas Day.

'Did you bring any money?'

'Times are hard, Angela. There aren't many jobs.'

'Are you joking?' she says, 'There's a war on. There's nothing but jobs in England. You drank the money, didn't you?'

'You drank the money, Dad,' I say.

'You drank the money, Dad,' says Malachy.

'You drank the money, Dad,' says Michael.

We're all shouting and Alphie starts to cry.

'Boys,' says Dad. 'Don't talk to your father like that.'

He says he has to see a man and he comes home drunk.

We have a sheep's head for Christmas dinner this year. Dad says he's not hungry and borrows a cigarette from Mam. 'Eat something. It's Christmas,' she says.

He says he'll eat the sheep's eyes. They're full of goodness.

'Yeuch,' we all say.

He drinks his tea, puts on his hat and picks up his suitcase. Mam can't believe he's going back to England on Christmas Day. He says it's a good day to travel. People think of Mary and Joseph and give you a lift in their cars.

He kisses us all and tells us to be good boys and say our prayers.

'I'll write,' he says to Mam.

'Oh yes, the way you always do.'

He looks at her, goes out of the door and pulls it shut.

# CHAPTER 11
## Laman Griffin

We have holes in our socks and shoes. We wear short trousers until we're fourteen. We wear the same shirt day and night. It's the shirt for school, for football, for climbing walls, for Mass. When I sit down in church, people smell the air and move away. If Mam gets a ticket for a new shirt at the St Vincent de Paul, the old shirt becomes a towel. It hangs wet over the chair by the tap for months.

We go to school through the lanes and back streets so we don't meet the boys from the rich schools. They wear wool jackets, school scarves, shirts, ties and shiny new boots. We know that they will go to university, take over the family business, run the government, run the world. We'll be the boys on bicycles bringing their letters and bread. We'll be driving lorries and bringing their coal. Our sisters will look after their children and clean their floors.

Grandma's neighbour, Mrs Purcell, has the only radio in her lane. I love the radio. On Sunday nights I sit outside her house and listen. You can hear plays by Shakespeare himself. Shakespeare's the best of all, even if he is English. He's as good as potatoes with butter. There are strange plays about Greeks too, who pull out their eyes because they marry their mothers by mistake. I want a radio.

We haven't paid for our house in Roden Lane for the past four weeks.

'I don't have money for one week. Where will I get money for four weeks?' says Mam. She sits by the dead fire up in Italy. There's no wood to heat water for tea until Michael pulls a loose bit of wood from the wall. 'One more bit and no more,' she says the next morning. She says that for two weeks until there's no more wall.

When the rent man comes for the four weeks' money, he says, 'God in Heaven, where's the other room? You had two rooms up here.
Where's the wall?'

'I don't remember a wall,' says Grandma, who's come to visit.

'I've been in this job for forty years,' he says, 'and I've never seen anything like this. Where's the other room?'

Mam turns to us. 'Do any of you remember a wall?'

'Is that the one we burned on the fire?' says Michael.

'That's it,' says the man. 'You're out. One week and you're out of this house.'

Grandma says she has no room for us, but our cousin Laman Griffin could give us a room. He's lived on his own since his mother died.

Grandma takes us to his house. It's two miles and it pours with rain all the way. Laman Griffin is in bed and there's a whisky smell. She wakes him up and tells him why we're there.

'All right, all right,' he says.

He moves to the floor above and we have the beds in the kitchen. There are no stairs in the house so we move the table to the wall. In the morning, Laman Griffin climbs down onto the table. He gets his bicycle and goes to work.

We explore the house. There are boxes everywhere, newspapers, magazines, bits of food, cups, empty tins. It's got its own toilet outside and a garden full of old stuff. 'Laman Griffin used to be an officer in the Royal Navy,' Mam tells us. 'But he started drinking and they threw him out. Now look at him. Dirty, working on the roads for the electricity company, living in a house that's a disgrace. He hasn't moved a thing since his mother died.'

We have to clean up so that we can live in this place. I

find a thick book called Pears Encyclopedia. I read it day and night. It tells you everything about everything and that's all I want to know.

Laman Griffin comes home at six every night except Friday, has his tea and goes to bed. On Fridays he comes home drunk. He brings his dinner in his coat pockets. A big piece of meat with blood all over it, potatoes and a bottle of beer. Mam cooks his dinner. He keeps his coat on, sits at the table and eats the meat with his hands. He cleans his hands on his coat. He's too drunk to climb up to his room, so he sleeps on the kitchen floor by the fire. On Saturdays he goes to bed at one in the afternoon and stays there till Monday morning. He lies in bed smoking cigarettes and reading books from the library all day. He throws money down for Mam to get his food. He throws down his library card for me to get his books.

***

Grandma fell ill after walking in the rain to Laman Griffin's. They took her to hospital and now she's dead.

The Irish Army is looking for boys who are musical. They want to train them in the Army School of Music. They accept my brother, Malachy, and he goes off to Dublin.

'My family is disappearing in front of me,' says Mam.

Laman Griffin doesn't climb down to go to the toilet. He uses a pot in his room.

'I have a job for you, boy,' he says to me one day. 'You'd like to help your mother, wouldn't you?'

'I would.'

'Well, that pot up in my room is very full. I want you to empty it in the toilet, wash it out and take it back up.' The first few times I do it I'm sick behind the toilet.

He says I'm a good boy. I can get a book for myself at the library and borrow his bicycle. He laughs and Mam looks at the dead ashes in the fireplace.

I'm nearly fourteen and it's June, the last month of school forever. Mam takes me to the post office to see about a job as a telegram boy. 'You can't start until you're fourteen,' says Mrs O'Connell, 'so come back in August.'

Mr O'Halloran tells the class it's a disgrace. 'Clever boys like McCourt, Clarke and Kennedy are thrown away in this free Ireland. You're too good to be telegram boys. You must get out of this country and go to America.'

Laman Griffin's house is not our house and we don't feel free in it. We have to be quiet when Laman comes home and goes to bed. We stay out until after dark, but then there's nothing to do.

Mam tells us to go to bed and read a book. 'I'll just take up Laman Griffin's last cup of tea and I'll come to bed myself.' There are nights when she never comes down. We hear noises. Malachy says it's too hard to climb down in the dark. He's only twelve and he doesn't understand. I'm thirteen and I know what they're doing.

In church the priest shouts at us boys. 'You must not have dirty thoughts and do dirty things to yourselves. It's a sin. When boys do dirty things, the Virgin Mary turns her face away and cries. Why does she cry, boys? Because the Holy Ghost lives in your bodies and you are making your bodies dirty. Every time you do a dirty act, you take a step closer to hell. Keep your hands to yourself and take a step back towards heaven.'

I can't keep my hands to myself. I pray to the Virgin Mary and tell her I'm sorry. I go to the priest and tell him I'm sorry, but he doesn't believe me. He tells me I must give up this terrible sin. I go from church to church looking for an easy priest. Paddy Clohessy tells me there's one who is ninety years old and can't hear any more in a church near him. Every few weeks I tell the old priest about my sins and he says I should pray for him. Sometimes he falls asleep and I don't wake him.

One Friday night Laman Griffin comes home drunk as usual. He tells my mother to make him some tea. She says there's no coal for the fire. He shouts at her, 'You great fat thing living under my roof for nothing with your horrible kids.' I want to hit him for the way he talks to my mother.

'Did you empty my pot?' he asks me.

'Oh, I forgot. I'll do it this minute.'

'You forgot,' he shouts. 'I give you twopence a week to empty my pot and you forgot.'

'He was at school all day,' says Mam. 'Then he had to see the doctor for his sore eyes.'

He tells her to shut up and she goes quiet by the fire. He tells me to shut up and go to bed.

'You're not my father. You can't tell me what to do.'

He pushes the chair back from the table. He sticks his finger between my eyes. He hits my shoulders and then my head. My mother jumps up and tries to pull him away.

'I'll kill you, you little beggar,' he shouts.

Mam is screaming and pulling at him. He falls back. 'Come on,' she says, 'he's only a child.'

He goes up to his bed. I expect Mam to come and put her arm round me. But she goes up to him.

I can't stay here. I leave the house. I dream about learning to fight and killing Laman Griffin. I go to Grandma's house. Since Grandma died, Uncle Pat has lived there on his own. He's sitting up in bed eating fish and chips. He says there's no food in the house, but I can sleep in Grandma's bed tonight.

# CHAPTER 12
## Telegram boy

It's the day before my fourteenth birthday and I see myself in the mirror. How can I ever start a job at the post office? All my clothes are torn. But if my clothes are bad, I'm worse. My hair sticks out, my eyes have yellow stuff at the corners, my skin is terrible and my teeth are black.

I have to look better than this for my job. I take off my clothes and wash them under the tap at the back of Grandma's. I hang them on the line. Other people's washing is bright and colourful and dances in the wind. Mine hangs from the line like dead dogs. I pray they'll be dry for tomorrow, which is the start of my life.

I have no other clothes so I stay in bed all day. It gets cold and I look for something to wear. All I can find is Grandma's old black dress. It smells of old dead grandmother, but I'm cold and no one will ever know.

That night Uncle Pat falls down drunk outside the pub. Aunt Aggie and Uncle Pa are called and they carry him home to Grandma's.

'What are you doing in this house, in that bed?' screams Aunt Aggie when she finds me. 'Get up and make tea for your Uncle Pat.'

I don't move because I'm wearing my grandmother's dress. She pulls back the bed clothes. She looks as if she's seen a ghost.

'Mother of God, what are you doing in my dead mother's dress?'

Uncle Pa Keating falls against the wall laughing. He tells me I look beautiful and black suits me.

I tell them I washed my clothes for my big job – telegram boy at the post office.

She sends me outside to get water in my grandmother's dress. Kathleen Purcell from next door is letting her cat out and sees me. The whole lane will know by morning. Shall I just stick my head out of the window and tell the world about myself and the dress?

The next day I'm fourteen. I put on my wet clothes and leave the house. I meet Aunt Aggie in the lane. She walks with me to the post office. She doesn't say anything. Is she going to tell them about my grandmother's dress?

'Go in,' says Aunt Aggie.

Mrs O'Connell and another woman are sitting at a desk inside. One is fat and one is thin. There are telegram boys sitting along a wall. I tell them I'm there to start work.

'What kind of work is that?'

'Telegram boy, miss,' I say.

'I thought you were here to clean the toilets,' laughs Mrs O'Connell. 'You're four days early. Today is Thursday and the job starts Monday.'

They all laugh at me as I leave and my face feels hot.

Outside, Aunt Aggie is waiting.

'Your clothes are a disgrace. They smell like dead birds.'

She takes me to Roche's Stores and buys me a shirt, a pair of trousers, two pairs of socks and some new shoes. She gives me two shillings to have tea and a cake on my birthday. Then she goes home on the bus.

I run down to Arthur's Quay with the new clothes under my arm. I look out at the River Shannon. I don't want the world to see a man crying on his fourteenth birthday.

At the end of my first week as a telegram boy, Mrs O'Connell gives me my money, a pound, my first pound. I want to wave my pound at the world. There he goes, they'll say, Frankie McCourt, the working man, with a pound in his pocket.

It's Friday night and I can have fish and chips and go to the cinema. I see my brother Michael across the street. He's hungry and wonders if there's any chance of a bit of bread. He wants to stay the night at Grandma's as it's a long walk back to Laman Griffin's.

'Don't worry about bread, Michael,' I tell him. 'We'll have fish and chips and lemonade, then we'll see James Cagney at the cinema and eat two big bars of chocolate.' He can't believe it.

We dance all the way back to Grandma's after the film. When Michael's asleep, I think about America. I have to save money for my ticket instead of spending it on fish and chips. If I don't, I'll be in Limerick forever.

***

School starts for Michael in September and on some days he stays at Grandma's. He's tired and hungry with two miles walk from Laman Griffin's and two miles back. When Mam comes to look for him, I can't look at her.

'How's the job?' she asks.

'Great,' I say.

We don't say anything about what happened at Laman Griffin's.

Sometimes she stays when the rain is heavy. Slowly she, Michael and Alphie move into Grandma's.

Now I have to give my pound a week to Mam. Some weeks she gives me two shillings for myself.

Malachy comes back from Dublin. He doesn't want to spend all his life in an army band.

We're all together again. We sit on the kitchen floor and eat fried bread and drink tea. We tell stories and talk about going to America.

I take thousands of telegrams to shops, factories, offices, priests, farms and the lanes. You never get a sixpence from a priest or a factory. The sixpences and shillings come from the lanes and from women who live on their own. Mrs O'Connell knows I like riding out into the country with telegrams, and she often gives me those.

One day I get the Carmody family telegram. The telegram boys know the Carmodys give you a shilling. So why am I getting it? I'm a new boy. Sometimes Theresa Carmody answers the door, they tell me. She's seventeen and she's dying of consumption. She knows there's little time left and she's mad for love. They don't want to catch consumption.

As I turn into the Carmody street I fall off my bike and cut my face. Theresa Carmody answers the door. She has red hair and green eyes like the fields around Limerick. Her skin is white.

'Oh,' she says, 'there's blood on you. Come in. I'll put something on your cuts.'

I don't know what to do. I don't want consumption. I want to be alive when I'm fifteen and I want a shilling.

She cleans my cuts and tells me to dry my clothes by the fire.

'Why don't you take your trousers off?'

'Ah, no.'

'Ah, do.'

I do. I hang my trousers by the fire. Soon we're on the green sofa and we're kissing. I'm thinking about consumption and I'm thinking if this is a sin, I don't care.

For weeks I take the Carmody telegram. Sometimes we lie on the green sofa together. At other times she's coughing too much. I don't tell the boys at the post office about the green sofa.

One Saturday I take the telegram. Mrs Carmody answers. Theresa's in the hospital, she tells me. She doesn't give me a shilling. I cycle straight to the hospital. I tell them I'm nearly fifteen and I'm her cousin, but they don't let me in. I go to St Francis and pray for Theresa. I tell him it was my fault, and anyway I love Theresa. Don't let her die and I'll never go near her again.

The next week she dies. I stand behind a tree and watch when they put her in the ground. I think Theresa will go to hell because of the green sofa. I want to tell the priest that I sent Theresa to hell. Lots of people have died in my family, but I never had a pain like this in my heart before.

# CHAPTER 13
## My first pint

The thought of Theresa in hell is driving me mad. I'm the worst sinner in Limerick. The weight of my sin is too much for me. I want to tell a priest about the green sofa, but I can't. A year passes but I can't do it.

There's a telegram for an old woman, Mrs Finucane. She asks me in and wants to know if I can read and write. She wants me to write letters to her customers. If you need new clothes for yourself or your child, but you don't have the money, you can go to Mrs Finucane. She gives you a ticket to a shop and they give you the clothes. She pays the shop less than the full price. You pay her back when you have the money - the full price and some extra. You pay her back weekly. But some customers don't pay her back. And they need letters.

'I'll give you threepence for every letter and another threepence if the customer pays after it. Come on Thursday and Friday nights.'

She has a book of names and addresses. Against each name, she writes what they've borrowed and what they have to pay. She shows me six names.

'Write to them,' she says. 'Frighten them.'

I show her the first letter.

'That's a good letter, boy,' she says. She asks me what some of the words mean. I write five more letters and she gives me money for stamps. I don't buy the stamps. Instead I keep the money. I run through the lanes of Limerick and I put the letters under the doors and pray that no one will see me.

The next week, Mrs Finucane is smiling like a cat. 'Four of them paid,' she says. 'Sit down now, and write some more. Put the fear of God in them.'

Week after week my letters get better. I use words I don't understand myself. The money makes her happy. She wants the Church to say Masses for her after she dies. Sometimes when I'm there, she falls asleep and her purse drops to the floor. I take a few extra shillings for the difficult words. I save my money in the post office.

Sometimes I have to write to neighbours and friends of my mother. I'm worried that they will discover me.

'That old Finucane woman,' I hear them say, 'sent me this letter with terrible words. Who writes those letters?'

'I would pull their teeth out one by one,' says my mother.

I'm sorry for their troubles but I need the money for America. One day I'll be a rich Yank and send home hundreds of dollars to my family.

I see a sign in an office window one morning. 'Clever Boy Wanted,' it reads. 'Good handwriting, good at maths. See Mr McCaffrey, Easons Limited.'

Mr McCaffrey says my writing is clear but he doesn't like my sore eyes. He wants to check with Head Office in Dublin about the sore eyes.

I start on Monday morning.

The next night is the night before my sixteenth birthday. Uncle Pa Keating takes me to the pub for my first pint. Uncle Pa lifts his glass and tells the men in the pub, 'This is Frankie, son of Angela Sheehan, the sister of my wife, having his first pint. Here's to your health and long life, Frankie. I hope you enjoy the pint but not too much.'

He tells me to drink it slowly. I listen to the men talk about the war and the poor Jews, and the little Jewish children and the piles of little shoes outside the gas chambers*.

*At the end of World War II, the world discovered that the Nazis had murdered millions of Jews in gas chambers.

Uncle Pa buys me another pint. The voices around me get louder and softer.

'Are you all right?' Uncle Pa asks. 'You've gone white.'

I want to go home. The air outside hits me and I can't stand straight. Mam is smoking a cigarette by the fire when I get home. 'Just like your father,' she says when she see me.

'I'd rather … I'd rather be like my father than Laman Griffin,' I manage to say. She turns away but I won't leave her alone. I've had two pints and I'm sixteen tomorrow. 'Did you hear me?' I shout.

She stands up. 'Don't talk to me like that,' she says. 'I'm your mother.'

She walks away and I follow her upstairs. I shout 'Laman Griffin, Laman Griffin' in her face till she pushes me away. I hit her on the face so that tears come into her eyes. I back away. There's another sin on my list.

***

In the morning I want to say sorry to my mother, but I can't.

'Do you want a cup of tea?'

'No.'

'It's your birthday.'

'I don't care.'

I go to the church of St Francis. St Francis stands there with his birds and animals. Why did I ever pray to him? He never did a thing. Why did he let Theresa die? Why did he let my mother climb up to Laman Griffin? I'm finished with St Francis. And the tears pour from my eyes. I'm so weak with hunger I could fall on the floor. And I cry out, 'Please God or St Francis. Help me because I'm sixteen today and I hit my mother. I sent Theresa to hell and I can't keep my hands to myself.'

There is an arm around my shoulder. A Franciscan priest. I feel like a child again and I rest against him, little Frankie on his father's knee.

'If you want to, my child, tell me your troubles.'

'I can't.'

'Then tell him,' he says, pointing to St Francis. 'And I'll listen.'

I tell him about Margaret, Oliver, Eugene, my father drinking all the money, my father sending no money from England, Theresa and the green sofa, not keeping my hands to myself, the little Jewish children and the shoes, not being an altar boy, my bad eyes, the tears in my mother's eyes when I hit her.

'God forgives you, my child,' he says. We pray together.

'But what about Theresa Carmody in hell?' I ask him.

'No, my child. Theresa is in heaven. The nurses in the hospital never let anyone die without a priest. You can be sure that she told a priest her sins before she died.'

Those words change my life. I run through the rainy streets of Limerick. I am so happy. Theresa is in heaven and her cough is gone.

# CHAPTER 14
## Robin Hood

I'm eighteen and I'm working at Easons and writing letters for Mrs Finucane. She says she's going to die soon. She puts money in envelopes and I take them to churches around the city. I give the envelopes to the priests and ask them to say Masses for Mrs Finucane.

I don't give them all the money. Why should I when I need money to go to America? I keep a few pounds for myself and save the money in the post office. I say a prayer for Mrs Finucane. Who will know?

I'll be nineteen in a month. I still need a few pounds for the ticket to America and a few pounds to have in my pocket when I get there.

One Friday night, Mrs Finucane sends me out for a bottle of wine. When I return, she is dead in the chair. Her eyes and her purse are wide open. I take seventeen pounds from her purse. I go upstairs where she has more

River Shannon

money under the bed. I take forty pounds and her book of names. On my way out I take the bottle of wine. It's a pity if no one drinks it.

I sit by the River Shannon and drink some wine. Aunt Aggie's name is in the book. She has to pay Mrs Finucane nine pounds. It might be the money for the clothes for my first job. Now she'll never have to pay it. I throw the book as far as I can into the River Shannon. I'm sorry I wrote those letters to the people in the lanes of Limerick, my own people, but they'll never have to pay now. I'm their Robin Hood and I wish I could tell them.

I go to get my ticket. A ship called the *Irish Oak* is leaving Cork in a few weeks.

'Nine days at sea, your own room, the best food, a bit of a holiday and that will cost you fifty-five pounds,' says the travel agent. 'Do you have it?'

'I do.'

I tell Mam I'm going in a few weeks. She cries. Michael says, 'Will we all go some day?'

'We will,' she says.

We have a party. Our first party. Mam saves a few shillings to buy bread, meat, cheese and lemonade. Uncle Pa and Uncle Pat bring beer and Aunt Aggie brings a cake full of fruit. She's made it herself. We sing sad songs.

'Is there any chance we can sing something lively?' says Uncle Pa. 'All this sadness will drive us to drink.'

'Oh God,' says Aunt Aggie. 'I nearly forgot. We must go out and look at the moon tonight.'

We all stand in the lane. We watch as the earth passes between the moon and the sun and the moon becomes dark.

'It's a bad sign,' says Aunt Aggie. 'The moon is practising for the end of the world.'

'The end of the world, my arse,' says Uncle Pa. 'It's the beginning for Frankie McCourt. He'll come back in a few years in a new suit, with fat on his body like a Yank and a lovely girl with white teeth on his arm.'

'I know, Pa, I know,' says Mam, and the tears run down her face.

## THE END

# From Book

***Angela's Ashes*, by Frank McCourt, was published in 1996 and was an immediate success. It has sold over four million copies and has been translated into 17 languages. When director Alan Parker read the book, he knew it would make a great film. In 1998, the filming of *Angela's Ashes* began.**

## The director

The film follows McCourt's book very closely. 'Frank's book is at the heart of this film,' Alan Parker said. 'I often told the actors to look back at the book, when they had questions. The film is very special –

Alan Parker with Frank McCourt

it is seen through the eyes of a child, but with the cleverness of a 65-year-old man.'

## The actors

Angela is played by **Emily Watson**. When Frank McCourt saw her for the first time, he said, 'That is my mother!' Before filming started, Emily stayed in Limerick for a few months to study the Irish accent. She also started smoking. When the filming was over, she found it difficult to stop.

Emily always has children around her in the film. She wanted Angela to be as real as possible. She carried real babies – never dolls.

Malachy McCourt, the children's father, is played by **Robert Carlyle**. He was already famous for his parts in the top British films *The Full Monty* and *Trainspotting*. But the part in Alan Parker's film was different. 'We wanted to show the different sides of Malachy,' Robert said. 'When I met Frank McCourt, he told me that he loved his father. I wanted to show this part of the man. He disappeared whenever things got difficult, but he wasn't a bad person.'

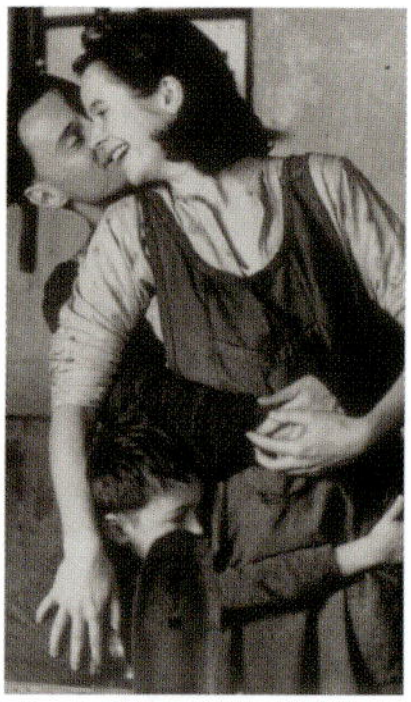

## The children

Over 15,000 children auditioned for the part of Frankie. Alan Parker needed to find three actors – a

# to Film 1

The three Frankies

young Frankie, a young teenage Frankie and teenage Frankie.

**Joe Breen** (5) played young Frankie. He had never acted before. His parents were farmers. Sometimes he had to milk the cows before he came to work! In the film, Joe has to eat a lot of porridge. He hated it!

**Ciaran Owens** (13) played Frank as a young teenager. We see Ciaran the most in the film.

**Michael Legge** (19) played Frank as an older teenager. 'I loved working on *Angela's Ashes*,' he said, 'but some things were hard. In one scene, I have to hit Emily (Angela). I found that very difficult.'

Everyone agreed that the children were the true stars of the film. 'They're so natural,' said Robert Carlyle, 'They did everything right first time!'

Alan Parker said, 'Children have to enjoy themselves when they're filming. They work better this way. I'm a friend first, and a school teacher second.'

**Work in pairs. Think of other books that have become films. Which ones have you seen? Which ones have you read? Compare the film with the book.**

**What do these words mean?**

**part publish translate doll audition scene**

# From Book

## The set

*Angela's Ashes* was filmed in southern Ireland; in Limerick, Cork and Dublin. Alan Parker travelled all over Ireland to find the right places for the film. It was difficult, because many of the old houses were no longer there. The McCourts lived in Roden Lane, in Limerick. The Lanes do not exist anymore, so the film studio built a new Roden Lane. It took six months. They used old photographs to help them.

'We wanted it to be a real picture of 1930s' Ireland,' said Alan Parker. 'We had to get a rain machine, because it used to rain a lot in Limerick. We tried to think of everything. In the book, Angela has a red coat which she wears for years and years. We made five copies of this coat for the film. It had to look older and older as the film went on. I don't know if anyone noticed, though!'

Back to school for Frank McCourt

When Frank McCourt visited the set, he was amazed. 'It's so real,' he said. 'It brings back so many different feelings. It's like meeting an old friend again.'

## Highs and lows

'Things were very hard, especially for my mother,' Frank McCourt remembers. 'But she could still make jokes.'

Malachy: *God is good.*
Angela: *God may be good for someone somewhere, but he hasn't been to Limerick lately.*
Malachy: *Don't say that. You could go to hell.*
Angela: *I'm there already!*

## Ireland and Italy

In the house in Roden Lane, there are two rooms. The children call them "Ireland" and "Italy". When it rains, the kitchen is cold and wet,

# to Film 2

like Ireland. So, during the winter, the family live in the room upstairs, where it is warmer.

Malachy: *It's like going on holiday to a nice warm country – like Italy!*
Angela: *It's more like Calcutta than Italy.*

## Irish dancing

When Frankie is ten, Angela wants him to go to Irish dancing lessons every Saturday. Frankie goes to one lesson, and that is enough! Instead, he and his friend go to the cinema. Every Saturday, when he gets home, Frankie has to show his mother his new dances. She soon realises that he has not been telling the truth.

Angela: *What dance is this?*
Frankie: *Err... 'The walls of Cork'.*
Angela: *That's not a dance*!

## America!

In many ways, the film has an optimistic ending. No one is sorry when Mrs Finucane, the money lender, dies. Frankie takes her book of names and throws it into the River Shannon. No one has to pay anything back. And now at last he has the money to go to America.

'I felt like Robin Hood in Limerick.'

**Discuss in pairs. What have you found out about life in 1930s' Ireland from *Angela's Ashes*?**

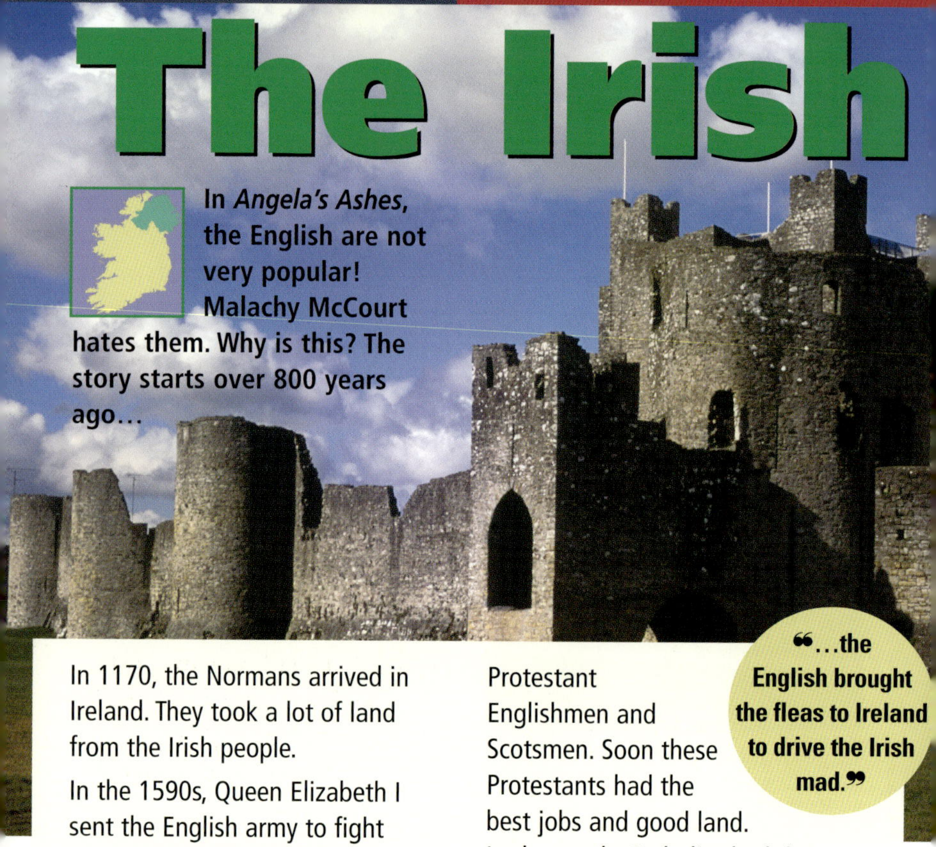

# The Irish

**In *Angela's Ashes*, the English are not very popular! Malachy McCourt hates them. Why is this? The story starts over 800 years ago…**

In 1170, the Normans arrived in Ireland. They took a lot of land from the Irish people.

In the 1590s, Queen Elizabeth I sent the English army to fight against the Irish. The English army won. Soon, English Protestants in Ireland ran the country.

Most of Ireland stayed Catholic, while England became Protestant. English kings were nervous about this. In 1607, many rich Irish men in the north of Ireland left the country to start new lives in Rome. The king of England, James I, gave their land to Protestant Englishmen and Scotsmen. Soon these Protestants had the best jobs and good land. In the south, Catholics had the worst jobs and poor land.

> **"Dad says he'll never help the English win a war."**

> **"…the English brought the fleas to Ireland to drive the Irish mad."**

For several hundred years, the most important people in Ireland were Protestant. They ran the Irish government in Dublin from 1782. But in 1800, this changed. The Prime Minister, William Pitt, wanted the English government to run Ireland from London. Many people in Ireland were unhappy about this, but in 1916, everything changed again.

# Question

## Easter 1916

On the morning of Easter Monday 1916, 1,250 Irish started a rebellion in the city of Dublin. They took several important buildings. The Dublin Post Office became the centre of the rebellion. They stayed there for days. The English fought back. Armies were sent and the Irish leaders were killed.

Dublin, 1916

But many Irish people wanted to continue fighting. There was a war against the British government which lasted for three years. Many Irish and English were killed.

## North and South

In 1921, Southern Ireland (Eire) became "free", with its own government. Most of the people there were Catholic. Northern Ireland chose to stay with Britain. Most of the people in Northern Ireland were Protestants. However, the Catholics in Northern Ireland wanted to be part of the south.

## Ireland today

The IRA (Irish Republican Army) wants Northern Ireland to be free from Britain. From the 1970s, the IRA attacked people in England and Northern Ireland. Many people died. But Irish Protestants in the north still want to stay with Britain. More than anything, however, the Irish people want a peaceful future.

**What do you know about your country's history? Write down five things that have changed its history.**

**Look up these words in your dictionary.**
**rebellion peace army Easter**

# PROLOGUE – CHAPTER 5

**Before you read**

Use a dictionary for this section.

1 Look at these words.

**bucket coal consumption flea porridge prayer whisky**

Which one ...

**a)** can you eat?
**b)** can you drink?
**c)** can you burn?
**d)** can you fill with water?
**e)** can you say?
**f)** may bite you?
**g)** is an illness?

2 Look at these words.

**saint priest beggar**

Who ...

**a)** works in a church?
**b)** asks for things but has no money to pay for them?
**c)** do people pray to?

3 Choose the right option.

**a)** When your eyes are **sore**,
**i)** they hurt. **ii)** they don't hurt.
**b)** Your **childhood** years are
**i)** age 0-12. **ii)** age 13-19. **iii)** age 16-20.
**c)** If you're a **disgrace**,
**i)** you've done something wrong. **ii)** you've done something well.

4 What do you think?

**a)** What is your idea of **hell**?
**b)** What is your idea of **heaven**?

**After you read**

**5** Answer these questions.

**a)** Why doesn't Angela enjoy Frankie's special day?

**b)** Why does Frankie wonder if Mrs Liebowitz could be his mother?

**c)** What happens to Angela a few days after they move to Windmill Street?

**d)** Why doesn't Aggie like Angela's children, do you think?

**e)** After Malachy mends Frankie's shoes, why does Frankie hide them in a bucket?

**f)** Why does the priest make strange sounds when Frankie tells him his 'big' sin?

**6** Write down words to describe ...

**a)** Frankie's mother. **b)** Frankie's father. **c)** Roden Lane.

# CHAPTERS 6 – 10

**Before you read**

**7** Find the best word for the spaces. Use your dictionary.

**stuff telegram typhoid fever tonsils**

**a)** People used to send urgent messages by ...

**b)** We have two ... at the back of our mouths.

**c)** Most of us have too much ... in our homes.

**d)** If someone is very hot, has spots on their body and pain in their stomach, they may have ...

**8** What do you think?

What three things would improve Frankie's life the most?

**After you read**

**9** Correct these sentences.

**a)** Most of the men in the lanes are on the dole.

**b)** At his flat, Fintan Slattery cuts his sandwich into tiny pieces and shares it with Paddy and Frankie.

**c)** Angela and Paddy's father have never met before.

**d)** Malachy won't help the war against Hitler after the Americans join.

e) Grandma and Aunt Aggie think Frankie looked after his family well when his mother was ill.
f) The big boys call Frankie names because he has a job.

**10** What was your first job? Did you feel like Frankie? Write about it.

# CHAPTERS 11 – 14

**Before you read**

**11** Write three good things that Frankie's father has done. Write three bad things.

**12** How do you feel when Frankie's father leaves his family with no money and no food at the end of Chapter 10?

**13** What do you think will happen to Frankie and his family at the end of this book?

**After you read**

**14** Answer these questions.
**a)** Why do Frank and his family have to leave their house in Roden Lane?
**b)** Why is Mr O'Halloran angry that Frank is going to be a telegram boy?
**c)** How do we know that Aggie cares about Angela's boys?
**d)** Why does Frank feel so bad in the church of St Francis about the things he has done wrong?

**15** What do you think?
**a)** Frank steals some of Mrs Finucane's money. Is he wrong or right to take it?
**b)** Frank and his friends get most of their information about the outside world from books, the radio and Hollywood films. Where do you and your friends get your information from?
**c)** Frank has dreamed of going back to America since he was four. Where would you most like to live?